WHAT'S THE BIG IDEA?

A ground-breaking series for young people which focuses on the hottest issues and ideas around.

Alien Life*
Animal Rights
The Environment
Food*
Genetics
The Media*
The Mind
Nuclear Power
The Paranormal*
Religion
Virtual Reality
Women's Rights

*coming soon

If you would like to make any comments on this book or suggestions for future titles, please write to us at:

What's the Big Idea?
Hodder Children's Books
338 Euston Road
London NW1 3BH

Cover picture: Nuclear Power Station, courtesy of Telegraph Colour Library

Published by Hodder Children's Books 1997

10 9 8 7 6 5 4 3 2 1

ISBN 0 340 69339 8

A catalogue record for this book is available from the British Library.

Printed by The Guernsey Press Co. Ltd., Guernsey, Channel Islands

Hodder Children's Books
A division of Hodder Headline plc
338 Euston Road
London NW1 3BH

WHAT'S THE BIG IDEA?

Nuclear Power

Felix Pirani

Felix Pirani

Illustrated by Christine Roche

Hodder Children's Books

This book is dedicated to the author's grandchildren:
Ben, Jason, Joshua and Nadine.

Contents

What's it got to do with me? 6
What is nuclear power anyway? 14
How did it all start? 28
Top secret 38
Hiroshima 44
Atoms for peace? 46
Chernobyl 54

What happens next? 60
What is this **Greenhouse Effect***? 64
Nothing left but the nukes? 74
What a waste! 76
Million year messages? 84
How exactly does it kill you? 90

What about fusion? 98
The wind, the Sun? 102
Amplify your energy 108

What the words mean 114
Who's who 118
Books for more information 120
Internet sites 122
Index 126
Thank you for helping 127

*__Greenhouse Effect__, and other words printed in bold are explained in **What the words mean**, which starts on page 114.

Nuclear power is one source of energy.

If something isn't done soon about energy supplies then when you're older:

- You'll have to survive global warming, maybe find a less agreeable lifestyle
- You may be paying enormous fuel taxes

- You may see the private car as an old-fashioned luxury
- You may be dodging more deadly dust like the fallout from Chernobyl.

WHO NEEDS ENERGY ANYWAY?

You need energy. Everybody does:

- to cook
- to make light at night
- to keep warm in winter and cool in summer
- to sow and harvest crops
- to mine and refine minerals
- to drive machinery and make things
- to clean up the environment
- to move people and things from place to place
- to run telephones, radios, televisions, hi-fis, computers, toasters, washing machines, traffic lights . . .

Where does it come from?

Humans have certainly been using their own muscle power, and have probably also been using energy from burning wood, since they first appeared on the Earth.

And they have been using:

- Animal power for at least ten thousand years
- Wind-powered sailing ships for at least five thousand years
- Water wheels and windmills for over two thousand years
- Coal, at least in Europe, since about 1200
- Oil from wells since 1860
- Mains electricity since 1882
- Electricity from nuclear power since 1957
- Electricity from solar power since about 1970.

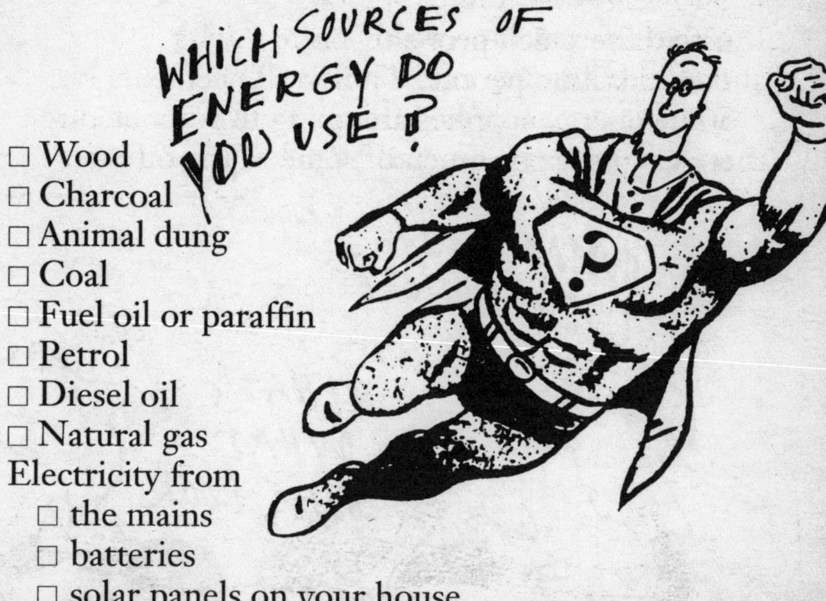

- ☐ Wood
- ☐ Charcoal
- ☐ Animal dung
- ☐ Coal
- ☐ Fuel oil or paraffin
- ☐ Petrol
- ☐ Diesel oil
- ☐ Natural gas

Electricity from
- ☐ the mains
- ☐ batteries
- ☐ solar panels on your house

Isn't there plenty for everyone?

There are a lot more people than there used to be and there are going to be even more in the future. Most of the extra people are going to be in poor countries.

In the middle of 1997 there were nearly 6 **billion** people on the Earth. That's 3½ times as many as there were 100 years ago.

By 2050 there will probably be about 10 billion people. They'll all need energy.

Some energy supplies are going to run out, and there can never be much of some of the others.

On average, people in rich countries use much more energy than people in poor countries.

Most of the Earth's population lives in poor countries. People in poor countries need more energy, not less.

People who haven't much energy available or can't afford to use much are probably going to stay poor
SO
many poor country governments have big plans to provide more energy for their people, and so eventually there will have to be more of it.

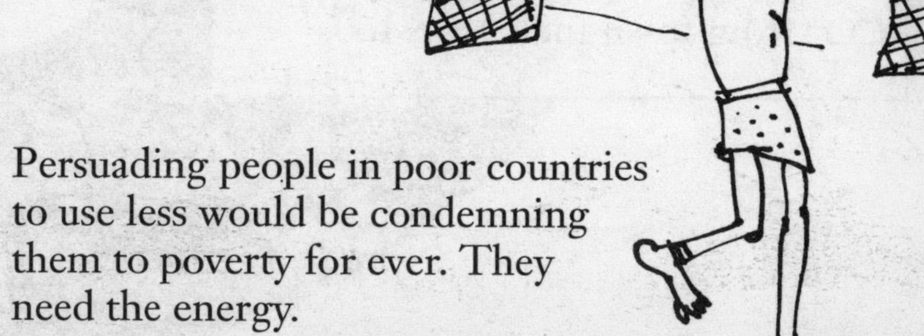

Persuading people in poor countries to use less would be condemning them to poverty for ever. They need the energy.

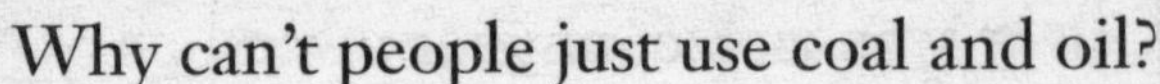

Coal and oil are **fossil fuels**. Burning fossil fuels contributes to the **Greenhouse Effect.**

CO_2 (carbon dioxide) from coal-fired power plants in China or anywhere else affects the climate everywhere.

Equally, CO_2 from burning coal and oil, and from motorcar exhausts in Britain contributes to the Greenhouse Effect everywhere. So eventually there will have to be less CO_2 from fossil fuels here, too.

So why not use water power and wind and solar cells and **biomass fuels**?

There aren't enough of those 'renewables' now, and probably won't be for at least a hundred years.

Nuclear power would be one way to get enough energy.

But **radioactive** gases from an exploding nuclear power plant in the Ukraine (or anywhere else) can increase the risk of cancer all over Europe, wherever the four winds blow.

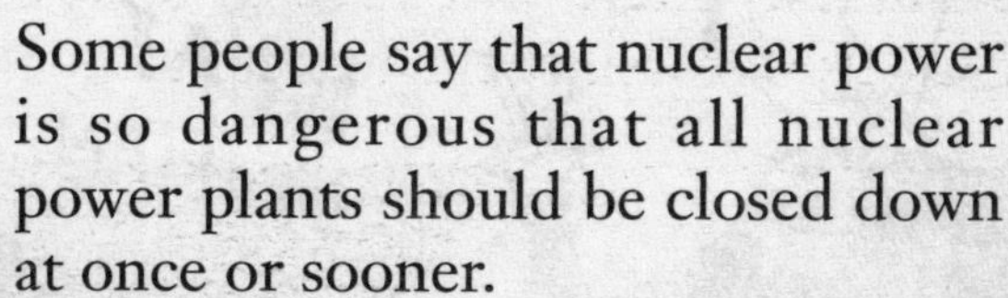

Some people say that nuclear power is so dangerous that all nuclear power plants should be closed down at once or sooner.

What is nuclear power anyway?

There are many other ways: coal, oil and gas can be burned, running water can be used to drive turbines, wind to turn windmills, or sunlight to heat solar panels.

Nuclear power is different from any of the others. It uses the forces that hold together the nucleus of the atom. Which creates...

One: Because nuclear forces are so strong, handling nuclear materials to release the power can be dangerous. Nuclear **radiations** from broken or unstable nuclei can damage living cells, so that these nuclei have to be kept well away from humans. If anything goes badly wrong, a lot of people can get hurt.

Two: Nuclear weapons – atomic bombs and hydrogen bombs – also use these forces. And the waste left over from nuclear power production can be used to make the weapons. So the more people have access to the power, the more could make the weapons.

Where does the energy come from?

Ordinary materials are made of atoms. Every atom has a nucleus*, which is roughly in the middle of the atom.

Nuclei, in turn, are made up of *nucleons*. There are two kinds of nucleons: protons and neutrons.

Some nuclei split into bits when neutrons hit them, and spit out more neutrons. Very occasionally, nuclei spit out neutrons without being hit.

This splitting into bits is *nuclear fission*. The bits are called *fission products*.

A nucleus which fissions may send out two or three neutrons in its turn.

Those neutrons may make more nuclei fission.

Which send out more neutrons.

Which make more nuclei fission...

This is a *chain reaction*.

*Nucleus is a Latin word meaning the kernel of a nut. Two or more are called 'nuclei'(which is the Latin plural of nucleus), not 'nucleuses'.

Every fission releases energy.

In a nuclear power plant, the fissions happen at a steady rate, under control, in an apparatus called a **nuclear reactor**.

Most of the energy coming from a reactor takes the form of heat, and can be used to turn water into steam. The steam drives a turbine, and the turbine drives an electric generator. In a fossil-fuel power plant, by the way, the heat is produced by burning the fossil fuel, but the rest of what happens is exactly the same.

If the fissions happen faster and faster, the result is an explosion. An atomic bomb is arranged so that the fissions do happen faster and faster, and the bomb explodes.

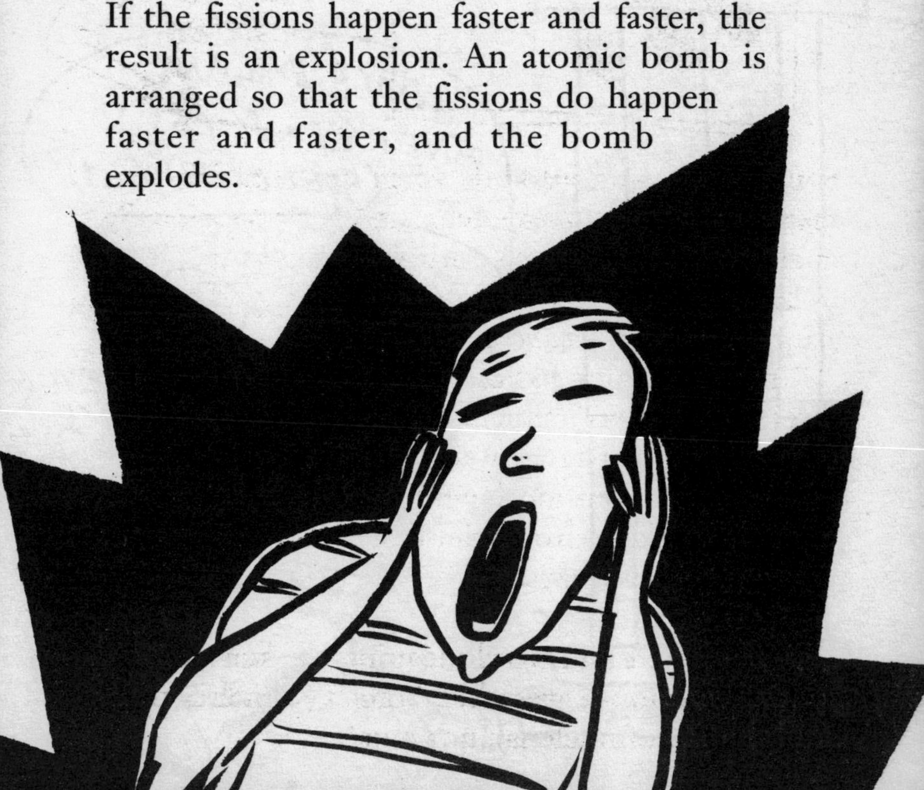

When a nucleus fissions, the total **mass** of the bits is less than the total mass of what there was to start with.

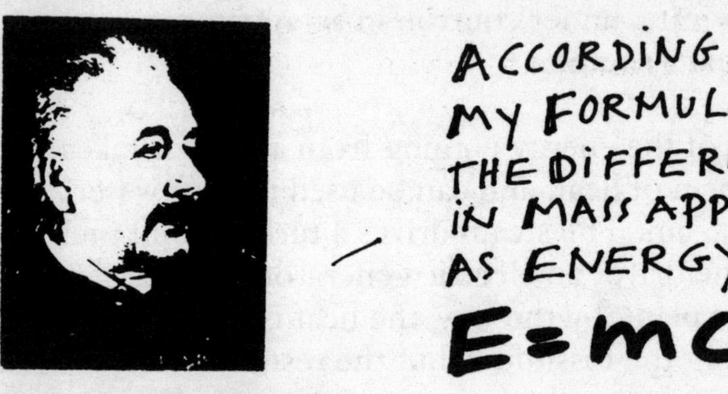

Suppose enough nuclei fission to result in a loss of mass of one gram*.

If they fission gradually, they will produce about as much heat as three thousand one-bar electric fires left running for a year.

If they fission within a short time, there will be as big an explosion as if about 20,000 **tons** of **TNT** had exploded.

* A LARGE TOOTH WEIGHS ABOUT A GRAM

What makes fission different?

In most ordinary materials, atoms are joined together into groups called molecules. Burning breaks up molecules and rearranges the atoms to make different molecules. A TNT explosion produces the same effects as burning, only faster. The nuclei of the atoms get moved around, but not broken up. But in nuclear fission, nuclei are broken into pieces.

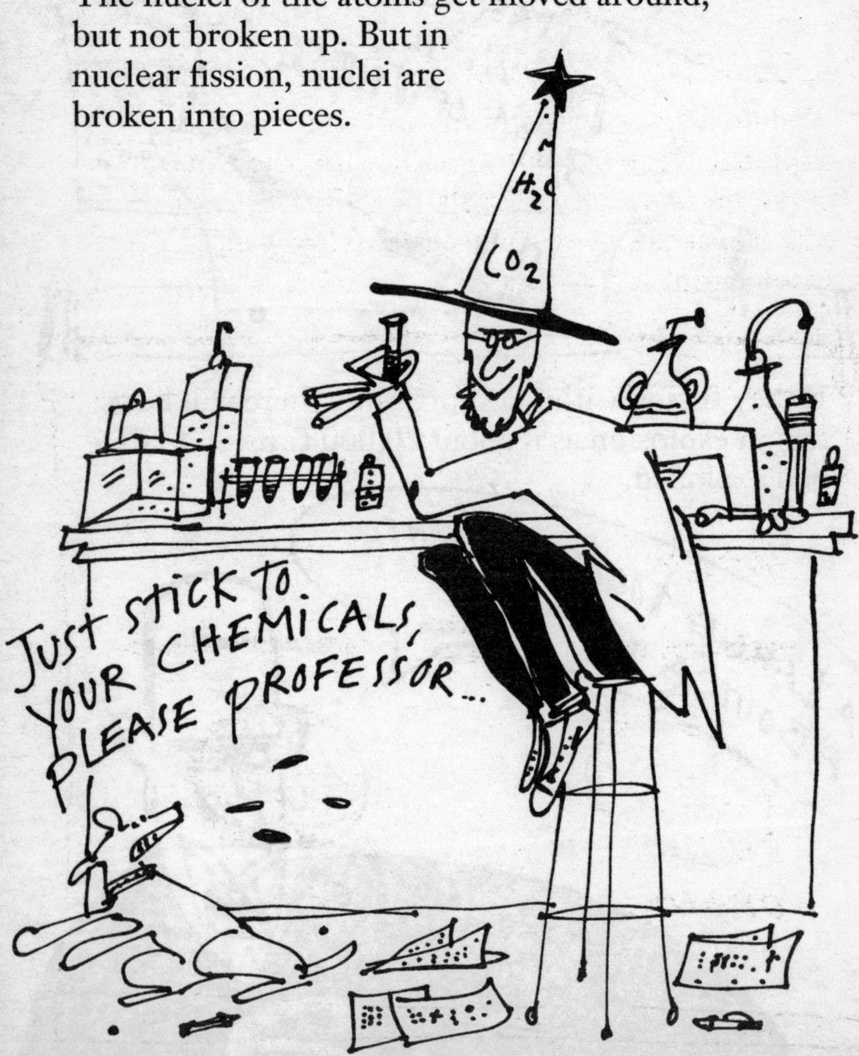

Around the nucleus of an atom moves a cloud of electrons.

The nucleus is several thousand times as heavy as all the electrons put together, but the electron cloud takes up about a million billion times as much space as the nucleus does. However, the whole atom is still tiny:

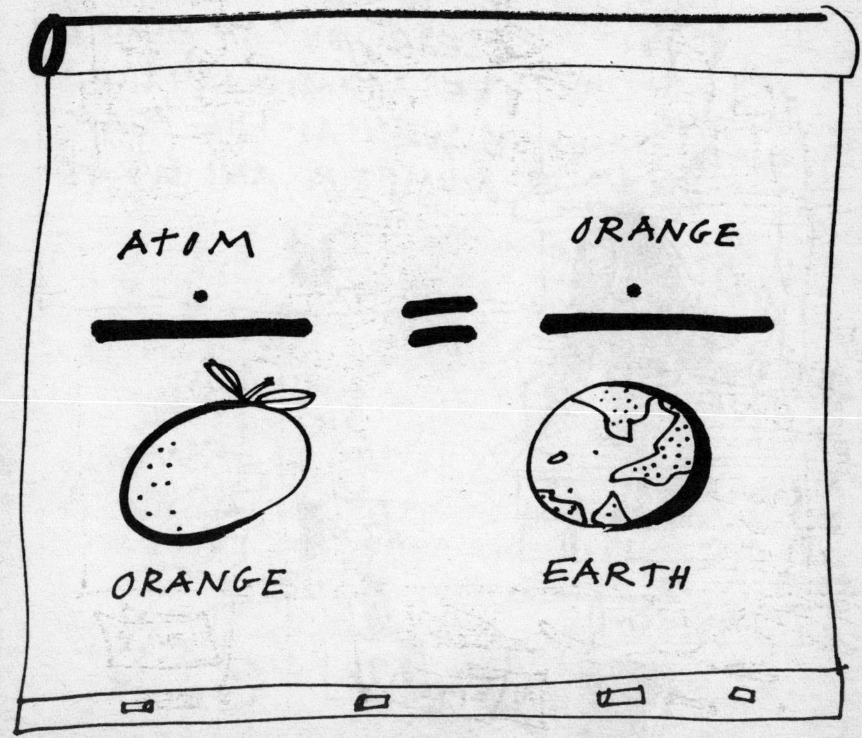

The numbers game

You can't fission any old nuclei. You have to have the right ones. The nuclei mostly used for fission power plants and atomic bombs are

uranium-235 and plutonium-239.

The number of nucleons in a nucleus is called the *mass number*. A uranium-235 nucleus – U-235 or ^{235}U for short – has 235 nucleons in it.

The number of protons, which is called the *atomic number*, tells you which chemical **element** it is. The atomic number of uranium is 92 – every uranium nucleus has 92 protons in it.

In any nucleus, nucleons = protons + neutrons and for $^{235}_{92}U$, 235 = 92 + 143.

There must be 143 neutrons, to make up the total of 235 nucleons.

Only 0.71% of naturally occurring U is U-235. Over 99% of uranium from a mine is U-238, which doesn't fission. And about one nucleus in every 18,000 is U-234, which doesn't fission either.

Quiz:

1. How many neutrons are there in U-238?
2. Pu is short for plutonium. The atomic number of Pu is 94. How many neutrons are there in Pu-239?

Answers: 146, 145.

However, if a neutron hits a U-238 nucleus, the nucleus may capture it, and turn into Pu-239, which does fission. Pu-239 can be used in power plants and to make nuclear weapons.

You can't just pick out the U-235 nuclei from the mined uranium and get rid of the rest, either.

Nuclei with the same atomic number (which means they're the same element) but different mass numbers are called **isotopes**. Different isotopes behave in almost exactly the same way when it comes to chemistry.

U-233, U-234, U-235 and U-238 are isotopes of uranium. It's difficult, complicated and expensive to separate them from each other.

It's easier to separate the plutonium from uranium, but dangerous, because plutonium is very poisonous, especially if you inhale it, or if it gets into your bloodstream through a cut in your skin. (Uranium is poisonous too, but not quite as poisonous as plutonium.)

What can I do about all this mess?
Try to understand what's going on. Discuss it with your friends.

To understand what's going on here and now, you need to know something about what has happened in the past, and what happens in other parts of the world.

Don't be NIMBY*. Think globally. You aren't living in a world where everyone can do as they like without affecting anyone else.

*Not In My Back Yard (do it somewhere else)

How did it all start?

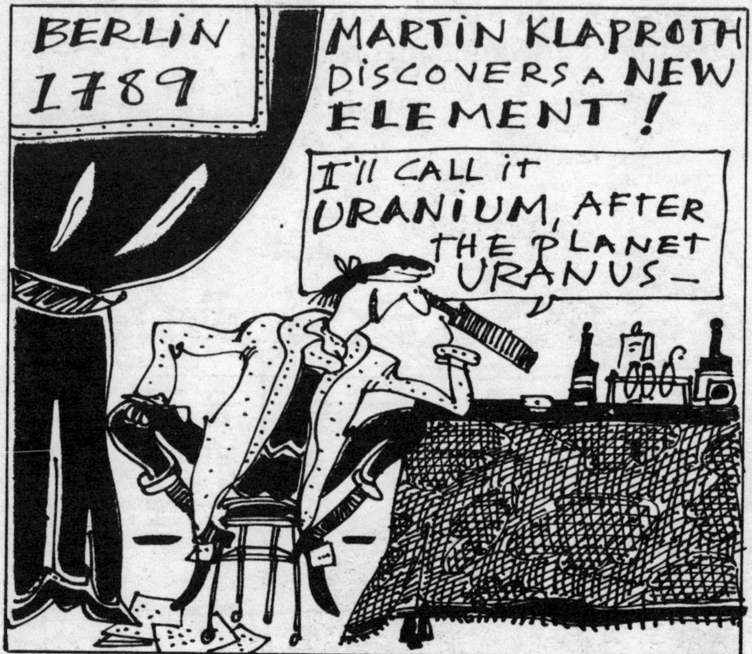

BERLIN 1789

MARTIN KLAPROTH DISCOVERS A NEW ELEMENT!

I'LL CALL IT URANIUM, AFTER THE PLANET URANUS –

PARIS 1898: MARIE & PIERRE CURIE

OÏE PIERRE!
I'VE FOUND TWO MORE ELEMENTS THAT PRODUCE RADIATION!
I'll CALL ONE OF THEM POLONIUM—
AFTER POLAND WHERE I WAS BORN.

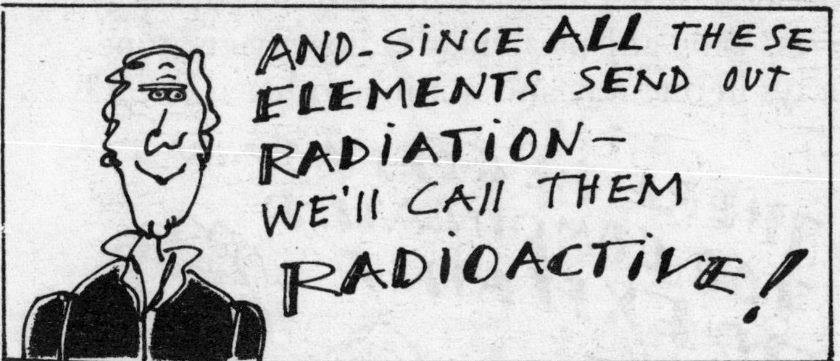

Those radioactive goings-on were produced by the transformation of one chemical element into another.

Three different kinds of radiation from nuclei were found:

Alpha rays or *alpha particles*, which are helium nuclei;

Beta rays or *beta particles*, which are electrons;

Gamma rays, which are electromagnetic **radiation**.

Alpha, *Beta* and *Gamma* are how you say α, β and γ which are the first three letters of the Greek alphabet.

The natural transformation of one radioactive isotope into another is *radioactive decay*. Often the transformed isotope itself decays, and what it decays into in turn decays, and so on. This is called a decay series. There are many different decay series. Why any particular radioactive isotope decays in one way and not in another is **TCTE**.

Here's one of the decay series* for uranium-238. It stops with Pb-206, which isn't radioactive.

$$
\begin{aligned}
{}^{238}_{92}\mathrm{U} &\rightarrow {}^{234}_{90}\mathrm{Th} + \alpha \\
&\rightarrow {}^{234}_{91}\mathrm{Pa} + \beta \\
&\rightarrow {}^{234}_{92}\mathrm{U} + \beta \\
&\rightarrow {}^{230}_{90}\mathrm{Th} + \alpha \\
&\rightarrow {}^{226}_{88}\mathrm{Ra} + \alpha \\
&\rightarrow {}^{222}_{86}\mathrm{Rn} + \alpha \\
&\rightarrow {}^{218}_{84}\mathrm{Po} + \alpha \\
&\rightarrow {}^{214}_{82}\mathrm{Pb} + \alpha \\
&\rightarrow {}^{214}_{83}\mathrm{Bi} + \beta \\
&\rightarrow {}^{214}_{84}\mathrm{Po} + \beta \\
&\rightarrow {}^{210}_{82}\mathrm{Pb} + \alpha \\
&\rightarrow {}^{210}_{83}\mathrm{Bi} + \beta \\
&\rightarrow {}^{210}_{84}\mathrm{Po} + \beta \\
&\rightarrow {}^{206}_{82}\mathrm{Pb} + \alpha
\end{aligned}
$$

Some nuclear transformations are much quicker than others. Suppose you start with a gram of one particular radioactive isotope. The time it takes for half of it to turn into something else is called the **half-life**.

- The half-life of uranium-238 is about 4½ billion years.
- The half-life of polonium-218 is about three minutes.

You never know which nucleus is going to decay next – all you know is the average time it takes for half of them to go. Why all this is so is TCTE.

*In the series, Bi is Bismuth, Pa is Protactinium, Pb is Lead (because the Latin for "Lead" is *plumbum*), Po is Polonium, Ra is Radium, Rn is Radon, Th is Thorium. + α or + β means that an alpha or beta particle comes out. → means turns into. The γ-rays have been left out.

What's U going to do next?

LEICESTER, SEPTEMBER 1933

PARIS 1933 – IRÈNE CURIE

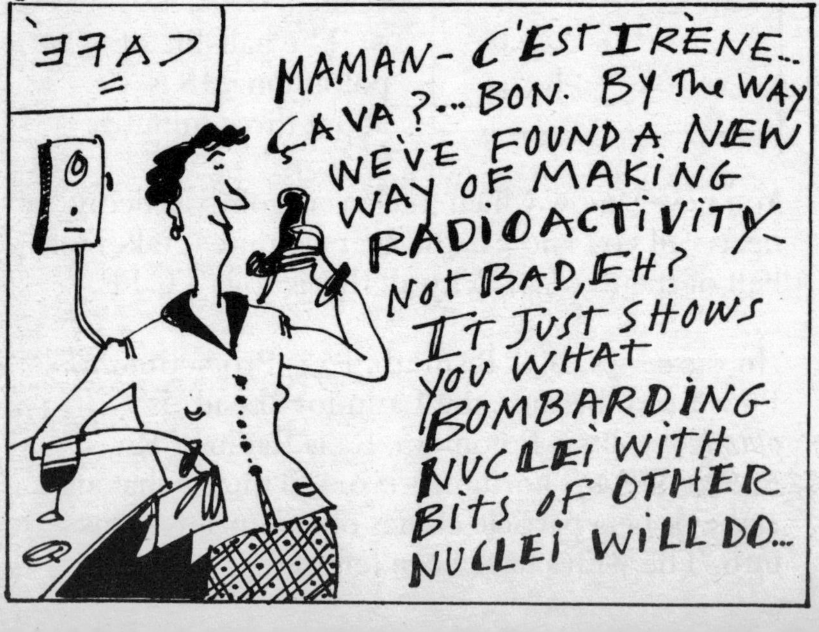

MAMAN – C'EST IRÈNE... ÇA VA?... BON. BY THE WAY WE'VE FOUND A NEW WAY OF MAKING RADIOACTIVITY – NOT BAD, EH? IT JUST SHOWS YOU WHAT BOMBARDING NUCLEI WITH BITS OF OTHER NUCLEI WILL DO...

The next year, in Rome, Enrico Fermi decided to try bombarding all sorts of stuff with neutrons.

Fermi thought that doing this created new elements, heavier than U.

WRONG!

Otto Hahn and Fritz Strassmann, working in Berlin, tried to check what Fermi had done. They couldn't figure out what was going on. From uranium they produced barium, whose nuclei are little more than half the size of uranium nuclei.

Going fission?

STOCKHOLM, 1939 – LISE MEITNER

NEPHEW – I THINK THAT WHEN THE U NUCLEUS CAPTURES A NEUTRON – IT STRETCHES OUT AND SHRINKS AROUND THE MIDDLE – THEN IT SPLITS INTO TWO –

SLOW DOWN, AUNTIE...

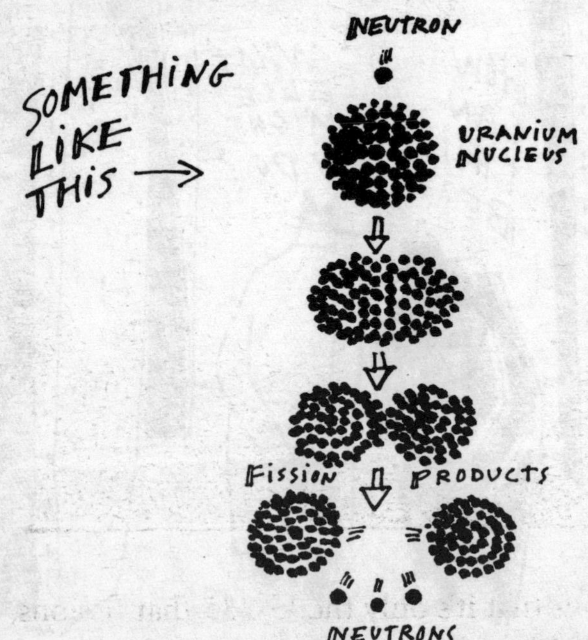

Otto Frisch: Let's call it

NUCLEAR FISSION.

It might release a lot of energy.

It turned out that it's only the U-235 that fissions, not the U-238.

Maybe there's a chain reaction

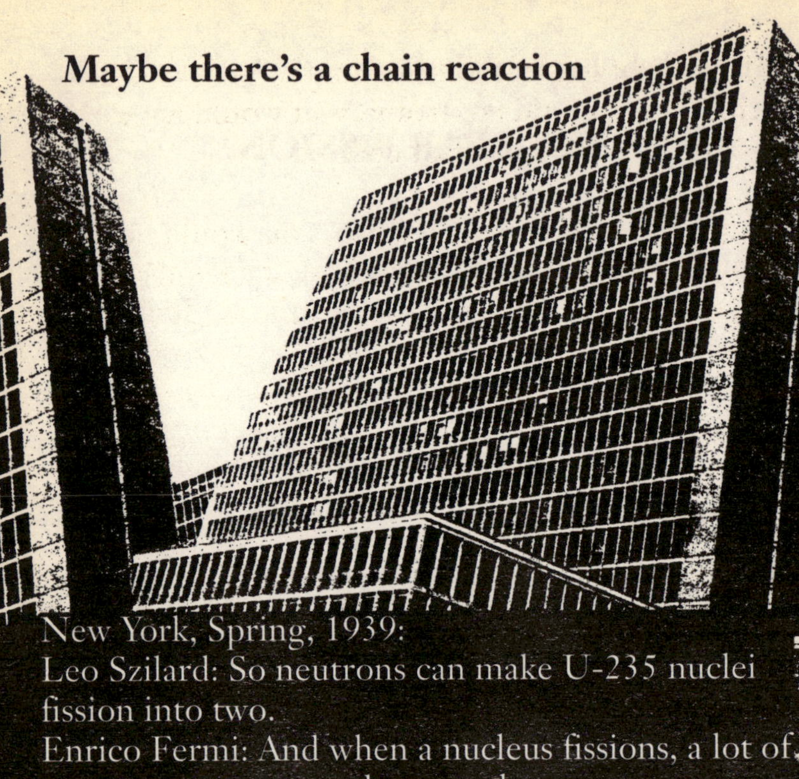

New York, Spring, 1939:
Leo Szilard: So neutrons can make U-235 nuclei fission into two.
Enrico Fermi: And when a nucleus fissions, a lot of energy comes out, and two or three more neutrons as well.

Szilard: Suppose that those neutrons were captured by other U-235 nuclei.
Fermi: Still more energy would come out, and even more neutrons.

Szilard: Suppose two came out for each one that was captured.
Fermi: It would be four the second time –

Szilard: and eight the third time –
Fermi: then 16, 32, 64, 128, 256, 512, 1024 and pretty soon millions and billions – a chain reaction!

Szilard: And an awful lot of energy.
Fermi: If you could control it, you would have a wonderful new source of energy.

Szilard: And if you just let it rip, you would have a very powerful bomb. This should be kept secret. There's going to be a war soon. Suppose Hitler found out.
Fermi: How can you keep it secret? Lots of other people are working on this.

Top secret

During the next year, elements 93 and 94 were first made. They were called Neptunium and Plutonium, because the two planets beyond Uranus are Neptune and Pluto. And $^{239}_{94}Pu$ fissions even more easily than $^{235}_{92}U$ does.

The US government started a big top secret nuclear bomb project. The Army was in charge. It was called the Manhattan Project.

The elements with atomic numbers 1 to 92 are found in nature. By 1995, elements with atomic numbers up to 111 had been made in laboratories.

In a squash court underneath a football stadium in Chicago, on 2 December 1942, Enrico Fermi started the first nuclear reactor.

They used to call reactors *piles* because they made them in a hurry by piling up the bits and they just looked like big piles of stuff.

Los Alamos, New Mexico, 1945:

'We'll have a bomb test in the desert. Then we can try out our other two bombs on the Japanese.'

Henry Stimson, Secretary of War: You are not to attack Kyoto. It was the ancient capital of Japan and is a cultural treasure.

Groves: This is a military matter. There are a million square feet of war factories in Kyoto.

Stimson: You are not to attack Kyoto.

Groves: What about Hiroshima, Kokura and Nagasaki?

Stimson: They're all right.

Scientists' bomb committee

Groves: We have to save American lives. We shall use the bomb as soon as possible, without warning.

James Franck: What about a demonstration in a desert, with representatives of the United Nations present?

Hiroshima

Hiroshima, Japan, 6 August 1945: A U bomb kills or injures about 140,000 people – over half the city's population. The bomb, called Little Boy, was carried by the Enola Gay. It had the explosive power of about 12,500 tons of TNT. Col. Paul Tibbets, the pilot, had named the plane after his mother.

9 August 1945: a B-29 called Bockscar, flown by Major Charles Sweeney, took off to drop the second atomic bomb on its primary target, Kokura Arsenal.

Bad weather made it impossible to bomb Kokura with any accuracy, so Sweeney headed toward his secondary target: Nagasaki. It, too, was under cloud cover. A small break in the cloud cover suddenly made visual bombing possible, and Fat Man was released. The Pu bomb – explosive power: 22,000 tons of TNT– fell 1½ miles from the aiming point. It killed about 70,000 people.

REPORT FROM COL. TIBBETS: There was the mushroom growing up, and we watched it blossom. And down below it, the thing reminded me more of a boiling pot of tar than any other description I can give it. It was black and boiling underneath with a steam haze on top of it. And, of course, we had seen the city when we went in, and there was nothing to see when we came back. It was covered by this boiling, black-looking mess.

Atoms for peace?

After the end of World War II, the United States went on building atomic bombs. Then in 1949 the Soviet Union tested an atomic bomb. After that, US scientists began to work on much more powerful bombs, called *hydrogen bombs* or *H-bombs*.

Hydrogen bombs release energy by joining nuclei together, instead of breaking them up by fission.

This joining together of nuclei is what makes the light and heat of the Sun and stars. It is called nuclear *fusion*. The bombs are called hydrogen bombs because the nuclei made to join together are the hydrogen isotopes deuterium (D or ${}^{2}_{1}H$) and tritium (T or ${}^{3}_{1}H$). An atomic bomb is used to start the fusion.

These bombs can have explosive power of millions of tons of TNT, not just thousands. So far, H-bombs haven't been used to kill people on purpose.

1 November 1952
An H-bomb with explosive power of about four million tons of TNT is exploded by US scientists.

8 December 1953
Dwight D Eisenhower, President of the United States (addressing the UN General Assembly):. . . this fissionable material would be allocated to serve the peaceful pursuits of mankind. . . abundant electrical energy in the power-starved areas of the world. . . the United States does not wish merely to present strength but also the desire and hope for peace. . .

1 March 1954
A US H-bomb tested at Bikini Atoll in the Pacific Ocean causes radioactive contamination over a 7,000 square mile area.

What about British nukes?

17 October 1956: The Queen opens Britain's first nuclear power plant: Calder Hall.

At first it was expected that nuclear power would be very cheap to produce, but as people worried more about safety, the cost of nuclear power stations went up and up, and British governments kept changing their nuclear plans.

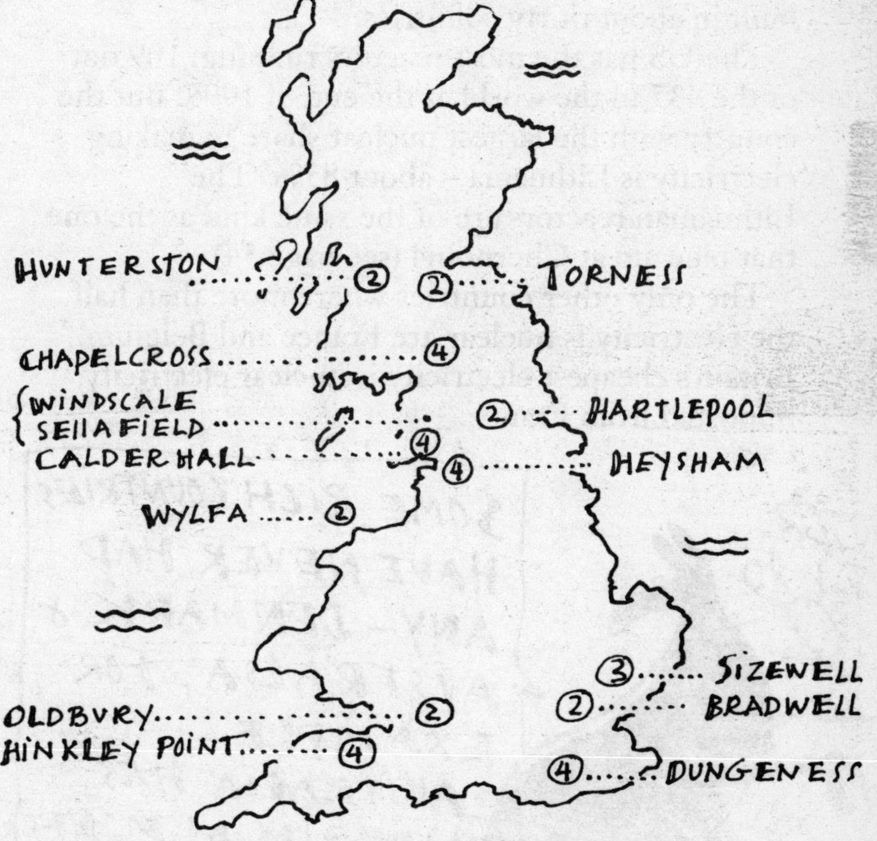

There are now 35 nuclear power plants in the United Kingdom, but there aren't likely to be any more for some time. In 1995 the electricity companies announced that no more reactors would be built.

Who else has nukes?

China, France, Russia, the UK and the US have nuclear weapons. India, Israel and Pakistan probably have. Several other governments could have them made quite quickly if they wanted to.

Nuclear power reactors are running or being built in about thirty countries.

The US has the most reactors running, 109 out of the 437 in the world at the end of 1995. But the country with the largest nuclear share in making electricity is Lithuania – about 85%. The Lithuanian reactors are of the same kind as the one that blew up at Chernobyl (see page 54).

The only other countries where more than half the electricity is nuclear are France and Belgium. Britain's cheapest electricity is nuclear electricity imported from France.

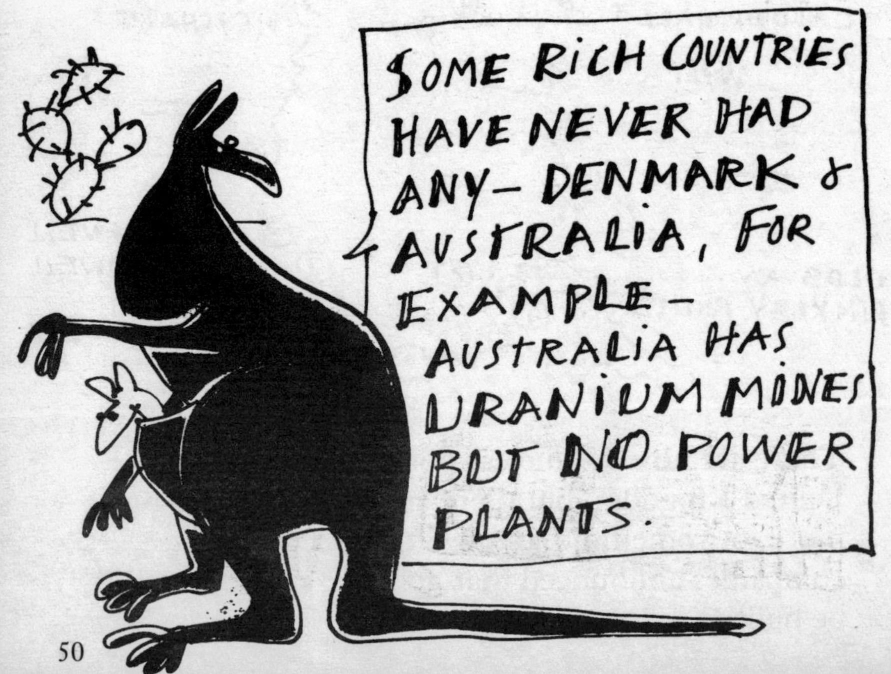

In Austria, a nuclear power plant was finished and ready for action, but was never used. Austrians so dislike nuclear power that their government offered free electricity to the Czechs if they'd close down some of their nuclear plants.

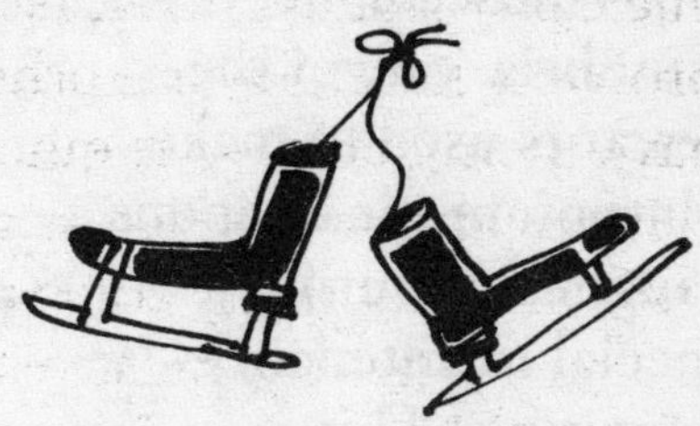

Italy used to have nuclear power plants, but closed them all down after a referendum vote in 1987. Italy imports quite a lot of electricity from France, so it's not really nuclear-power-free.

India was the first poor country to have nuclear power: ten plants, and four more being built. Pakistan has one, China three. China plans to have eight more by 2000. No African country has nuclear power except South Africa.

Don't drink the milk
10 October 1957
At Windscale, in Cumbria, one of the reactors used to make plutonium for weapons caught fire during a special maintenance operation. This couldn't be kept secret.

It took about two days to put out the fire.

Around 800,000 billion **becquerels** of iodine-131 escaped into the atmosphere, as well as some other radioactive isotopes.

Nobody knew just how the maintenance operation would go, and there was no rule book.

The report on what had happened was censored, because the Prime Minister, Harold Macmillan, was afraid that the Americans would refuse to make a nuclear cooperation agreement.

The following year the UK and the US signed an Agreement for Cooperation on the Uses of Atomic Energy for Mutual Defence Purposes.

Chernobyl, Ukraine: 25 April 1986

BANG

Reactor power went up to 100 times its normal level.

A steam explosion blew open the reactor core. The roof of the building collapsed.

About 4 billion billion becquerels of radioactive material escaped into the air.

Thirty one people, mostly volunteers who helped clean up the mess, not members of the public, died of injuries or radiation sickness within a few weeks.

135,000 people were evacuated from the area.

Chernobyl is still with us

At Chernobyl, a lot of rules were broken. The reactor was badly designed, but the people running it didn't know enough about that to realise that what they were doing was so dangerous.

The children

There has been an explosive increase in thyroid cancer in young children around Chernobyl, particularly in Belarus. Scientists associate this with the Chernobyl explosion.

The World Health Organization recommended that iodine tablets be made available to all school children in Europe. If there is another accident, they can take the tablets to stop their thyroids from absorbing the radioactive iodine that may be released.

In April and May 1996, firemen passed out iodine tablets to 400,000 people living near nuclear power stations in France, in case there should be an accident. Similar steps had already been taken in Austria and Czechoslovakia.

Three Mile Island

There have been many other power station accidents, but none as bad as Chernobyl. The Three Mile Island accident is a well-known one.

The Three Mile Island power plant is in Middletown, Pennsylvania. On 28 March 1979, a power reactor **coolant** pump broke down. Some valves that should have been open had been left closed, and one that should have closed didn't – but its indicator light showed that it had.

As a result, the operators made mistakes, and a lot of the core melted. Nearly all the radioactivity was kept inside the reactor building, so that very little damage was done, except to the reactor, which was a wreck.

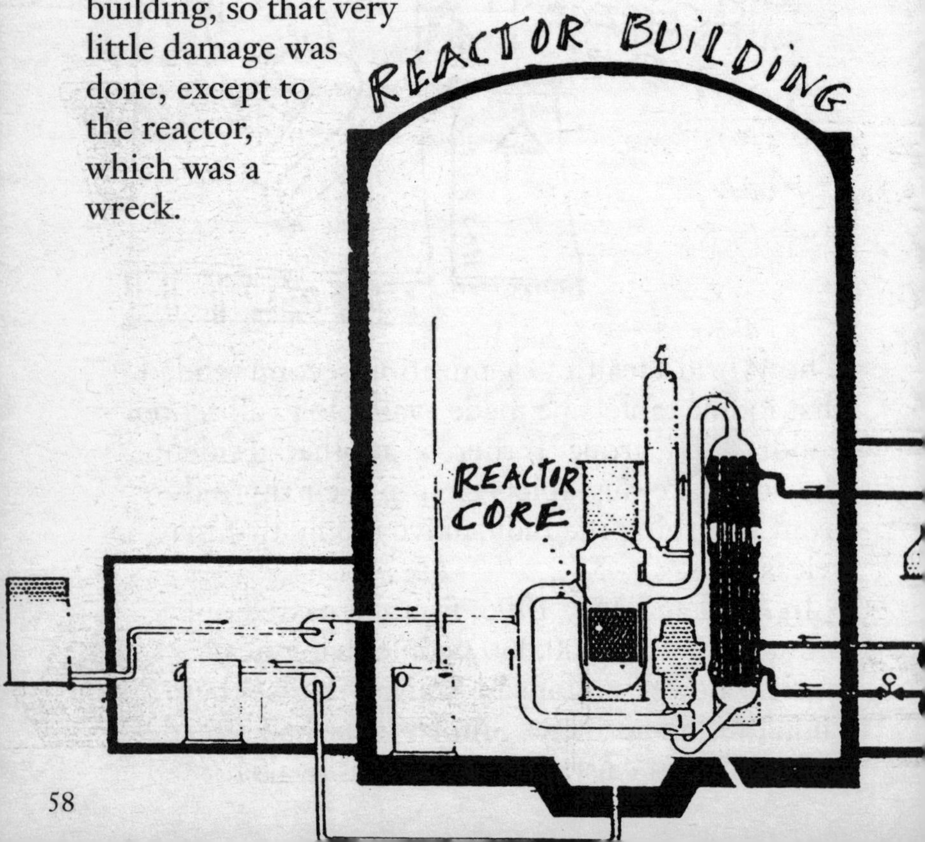

It is very likely that much safer reactors could be built. One idea is to put the whole reactor in a big concrete tank full of cold water. The water would have a lot of boron-10 in it.

Boron is good at absorbing neutrons. The idea is that if anything went wrong with the coolant supply, the boron-10 water would flow into the core and the reactor would shut down automatically without human intervention.

But you can't tell if it really works until you've tried it out, and besides, the reactors would be more expensive, so that the electricity would be more expensive, and so power companies don't want to build these reactors.

What happens next?

Nearly twenty percent of the world's electricity is made with nuclear power. Making it all from coal or oil would speed up the Greenhouse Effect.

Can't everyone use less energy?
Most people in rich countries could manage with less energy. And so they could save money, too.

They wouldn't have to do without things they are used to – just change their lifestyles a little:

- Paint house roofs white and plant shade trees, so as to be able to use less air-conditioning
- Use compact, fluorescent light bulbs
- Modernise water heaters
- Use public transport and bicycles and stuff like that.

But there are problems. Why should the landlord pay for a better water heater when it's the tenant who pays the electricity bill?

Poor people use a lot less energy than rich people. But most people in poor countries need more energy.

They need:

- better food
- health care
- schools
- proper housing
- clean water
- sewage treatment

You name it, they need it. And they need more energy to get it.

Using less energy is probably one reason why poor people:

- live less healthily
- get less education
- stay poor, die younger. . .

The energy used per person in the United Kingdom is about six times as much as it is in China.

Look at this graph. It shows how much energy is used per person in different countries, and how long babies born in those countries can expect to live.

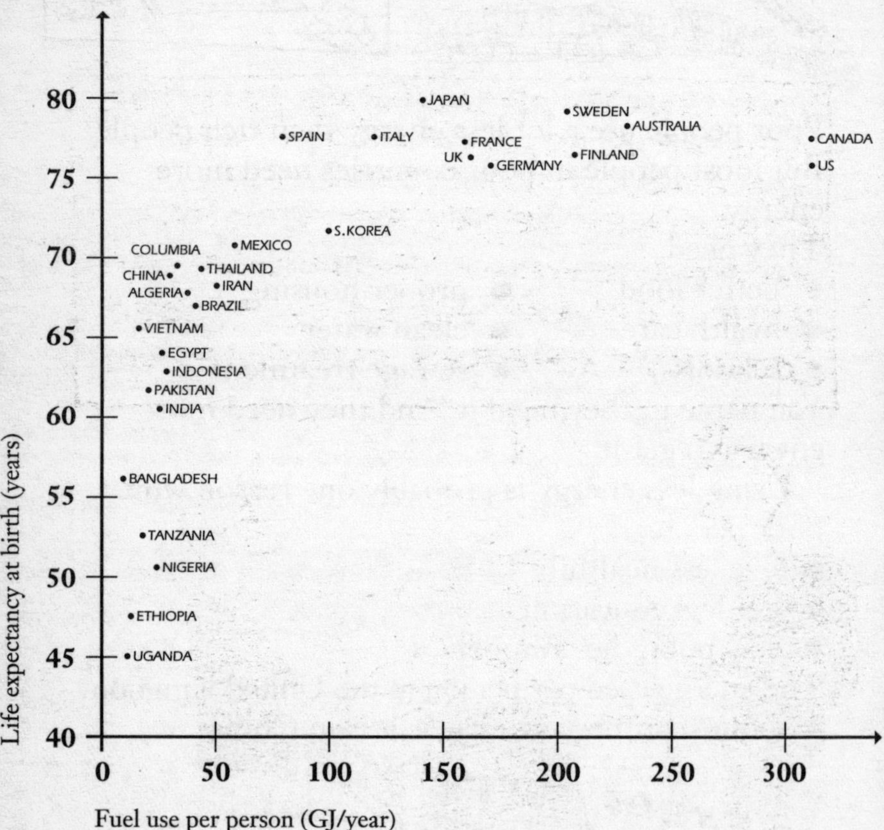

With few exceptions, people live longer in countries where more energy is used. Life expectancy – the average number of years that a newborn baby can expect to live if conditions do not change – keeps going up until energy consumption per person reaches about 70 **gigajoules** (GJ) a year.

After that it doesn't make much difference.

So more energy is needed, but it would be better if it does not come from fossil fuels, because of the Greenhouse Effect.

What is this Greenhouse Effect?

The Greenhouse Effect is a warming of the Earth's atmosphere that is partly the result of human activities, especially the burning of fossil fuels. It is not the heat from the burning that causes the warming, but the waste gases from the burning that make the atmosphere behave differently.

The Earth is warmed by light and heat from the Sun. Light and heat are forms of energy. The Earth in its turn emits (sends out) heat. The light and heat energy that the Earth receives is balanced by the heat energy it emits.

The Earth's atmosphere lets most of the sunlight in, but does not let all the heat out.

Some of the trapped heat comes back down to the Earth's surface, and warms the Earth some more. This is the *Greenhouse Effect*.

It's called that because the trapping of heat by the gases in the Earth's atmosphere is something like the trapping of heat by the glass walls and roof of a greenhouse.

There has always been *some* Greenhouse Effect in the atmosphere, and the Earth would be a very cold place if there weren't, but there is more now than there used to be, because there are more greenhouse gases trapping heat than there used to be. It's the extra heat that matters.

What does it?

The most important of the greenhouse gases that trap the heat is carbon dioxide (CO_2). Burning practically anything except hydrogen – wood, coal, natural gas, petrol or oil for example – produces CO_2.

Some of the CO_2 dissolves in the oceans. Some more is taken up by plant life. What is left over stays in the atmosphere.

Deforestation – cutting down forests so as to use the land for something else – means less plant life, so that more CO_2 will be left over in the atmosphere, and the Greenhouse Effect will get worse.

The warming

There is about 30% more CO_2 in the atmosphere than there was before the Industrial Revolution, when humans began to burn stuff on a large scale.

So more heat is trapped, and climate scientists say that the extra warming of the Earth – the *global warming* – that results is beginning to be noticeable.

It has been calculated that because of the Greenhouse Effect the world average temperature is likely to increase by between about 1° and 3.5°C during the 21st century.

This may not sound like much, until you compare it with the change in the world average between the middle of an ice age and the warm period between ice ages – only 5° or 6°C .

What could happen

Sea level is likely to rise as a result of global warming. Best guess: about 50 cm by 2100. It will probably keep on going up after that. Some islands will be almost submerged.

There are likely to be more extremely hot days and fewer extremely cold days. In some places more severe droughts or floods should be prepared for. The number of people in danger from flooding would double, from 46 million to 92 million, if sea level went up 50 cm. There may be more heavy rainstorms.

Changes in the weather are expected to be most damaging in countries nearer to the equator, which are generally poor countries.

Deserts are expected to become more deserty. Some forests may disappear. In some places different crops may have to be grown.

There's plenty which isn't known about the climate, so there's always the possibility of surprises, not necessarily pleasant ones.

The way the water circulates in the North Atlantic Ocean makes it several degrees warmer than it might otherwise be. It seems to have been very different in the past. If there were a sudden change, Europe might become a much *colder* place than it is now, despite the 'global warming'!

Who did it, and who should pay?

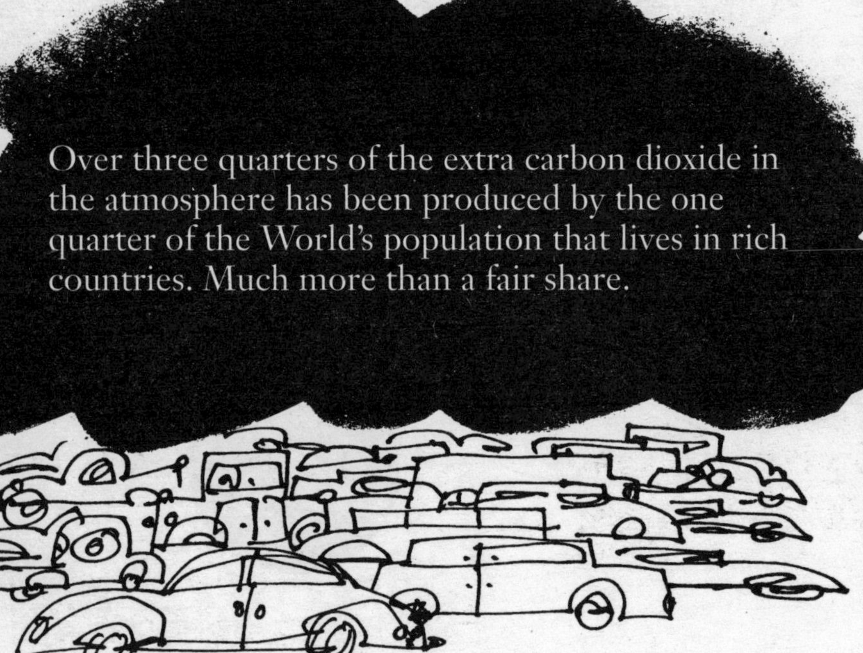

Some people say that people in rich countries should be the ones to produce less CO_2, because they have been producing more than their share for so long, and are largely responsible for the global warming mess that the world is in.

Others say that it is mainly people in poor countries who should produce less, because there are so many of them that changes they make will have greater effect.

Some people say that rich countries should pay poor countries to produce less carbon dioxide.

People in poor countries say that they don't see why they should produce less, especially since producing more carbon dioxide seems to be necessary to become less poor.

They say that they deserve to be paid anyhow, because one reason that rich countries are rich is that they have taken so much wealth from poor countries without paying for it.

Fossil fuels won't last for ever

If fossil fuels go on being used up no faster than they are used now and more expensive supplies are not considered, then the supplies of important fossil fuels left on the Earth are only:

45 years of oil
60 or 65 years of natural gas
170 to 200 years of hard coal, and
300 to 400 years of brown coal.

At present, about three-quarters of the world's total energy is produced from fossil fuels. About 5% is nuclear, and 5% is hydroelectric. Most of the rest is produced by burning wood and other biomass fuels.

Some electricity is produced from the wind, and some by capturing sunlight directly, but the amounts are quite small, and they aren't likely to get bigger for some time (see page 102).

Hydro-electric power is produced by building a dam across a river and controlling the flow of water arriving at the dam so that it drives turbines which turn electricity generators.

Probably two or three times as much hydro-electric power could be produced, but only if some large dams were built.

Large dams need large reservoirs, which means inundating a lot of land, and sometimes displacing a lot of people. If the Three Gorges hydro-electric project in China, with the largest dam in the world, goes ahead, more than a million people will have to move.

Nothing left but the nukes?

There are other possibilities besides nuclear power. Many people think that solar power – making electricity directly from sunlight, is the most promising, but it's expensive. It will probably become much cheaper and be used more widely as the technology is developed.

The big problem about solar power, if you use nothing else, is that it's only sunny in the daytime.

What can be expanded now is nuclear power, although it too has its problems: ACCIDENTS, WASTES, WEAPONS. The great advantage of nuclear power is that power plants could be built now, without the need for a lot more research.

The main accident risk with reactors is the core.

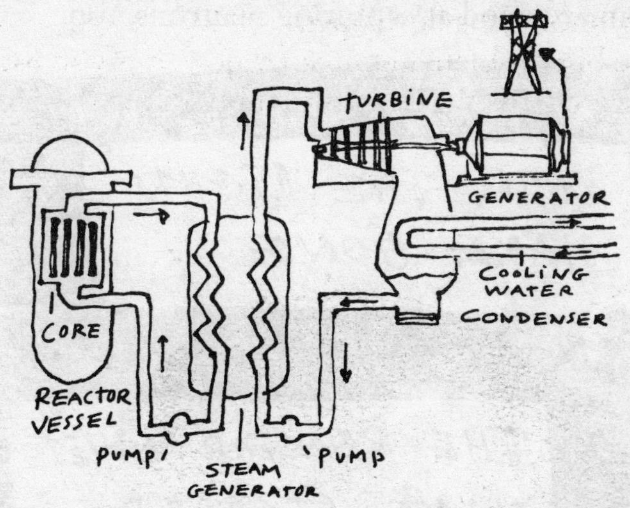

Every reactor has a coolant to carry away the heat produced by fission. The coolant is usually either water or a gas. If something goes wrong with the coolant supply and the core does get too hot, some radioactive stuff may escape. Even if that happens, the reactor building may be able to keep the radioactivity in.

What a waste!

When a U or Pu nucleus in a reactor core fissions, it spits out a few neutrons and splits into two lighter nuclei, the fission products. Most of the neutrons are needed to produce more fissions, but the fission products are all radioactive, and many of them are good at capturing neutrons, too.

If nothing were done about this, then after a while the fissioning would slow down because of a shortage of neutrons, and eventually the reactor would stop altogether. This is the main reason why the fuel has to be replaced every few years.

The 'spent fuel' has to be taken out of the reactor when only about 3% of the U has been used.

In some countries, including the UK, the remaining U, and some Pu, is separated from the waste fission products and used to make new fuel. This is called *reprocessing*.

But there is still some waste. This is **'high level waste'** (HLW).

In other countries, including the US, all the spent fuel from power plants is considered to be high level waste, and there is no reprocessing.

Danger – radioactive!

Either way, HLW is radioactive and dangerous.

Then there's 'intermediate level waste' (ILW) – fuel cans and used reactor bits, for example, and 'low level waste' (LLW), such as protective clothing, paper towels and cardboard.

How much is there?

Suppose you spread one year's British radioactive waste out evenly over a football pitch, in three layers, one on top of the other. There would be:

What's done with it?

In Britain, some liquid LLW is drained into the sea; solid LLW is stored in a trench and a concrete vault at Drigg, near Sellafield* reprocessing plant in Cumbria. ILW is packed in cement in 500-litre drums at Sellafield.

More than 95% of the radioactivity in nuclear power plant wastes is in the HLW. In Britain it is a liquid, left over from reprocessing, which is made into $1\frac{1}{2}$ ton glass blocks at Sellafield. This is called *vitrification*.

> Some people say that vitrification of waste containing elements that could fission is like creating atomic bomb ores for the future.

All nuclear waste becomes less radioactive with time – after one **half-life** of some isotope has passed, the radiation from nuclei of that isotope is reduced by half.

*The Sellafield plant was renamed Windscale in 1947, when plutonium production was started, to avoid confusion with another nuclear plant called Springfields, in Lancashire. The Windscale reactors were closed after the accident (see page 52), and the name isn't used for the plant any more. No wonder.

Some of the radioactive nuclei in the waste, generally elements with high atomic numbers, have long half-lives. Some others, generally the fission products, have short half-lives.

The big PROBLEM is that waste contains some nuclei whose half-lives are millions of years. This means that it has to be stored for a long time before being put where it might escape into the environment and injure people.

The British government's present idea is to store the vitrified waste for at least 50 years. They haven't decided what should be done with it after that, but say that burying it might be best.

One nuclear industry bigshot suggested that it could be left safely for thousands of years in an above ground 'glass pyramid' near Sellafield. Cumbria county officials didn't seem to like that idea. Many people are NIMBY about nuclear waste.

Yucca mountain and all that

Many people think that in deciding what to do with long half-life nuclear wastes, it is important to make sure that the risks to future generations are as small as possible.

They say that it would be wrong to do nothing – that simply leaves all the responsibility for sorting out the wastes to your descendants. But the descendants should still be left some choice about what to do with them.

Some people have come to the conclusion that the best thing to do is to bury the wastes deep in the ground, in a place where the right conditions for storage will last. It might be even better to bury them at sea, but that idea is not at all popular.

In the US, where people are extremely NIMBY, the only place for burying wastes that has been found so far is near Yucca Mountain in Nevada. The underground conditions there are still being studied.

People don't agree on how much time is needed for safe storage; a US government committee says ten thousand years, but a committee of scientists thinks that a million years would be better. Perhaps international supervision would be needed.

Why ten thousand years? By then another Ice Age may be beginning, and no-one can tell what the conditions underground are likely to be, after that.

Why a million years? Some isotopes go on being dangerously radioactive for as long as that.

Some people ask whether it is right to create this danger just to maintain an energy-wasteful lifestyle.

Million year messages?

However nuclear waste is stored, people of the future should be warned about it. How do you leave a warning message that will still be understood ten thousand years from now? Or a million?

Languages change – you wouldn't understand much of what was spoken and written in England a thousand years ago, without being taught how, let alone ten thousand years ago.

Written records fall to pieces – the oldest known clay tablets are only about five thousand years old.

The meaning of great monuments is forgotten – the building of Stonehenge began only about four thousand years ago, but people who have spent years studying it cannot agree what it was for.

Some say that each nuclear waste site should be surrounded by great stone pillars with warning messages engraved on them in all the languages of the United Nations.

Others say that the safest location for the message would be on an artificial satellite, not near to the waste site at all.

Some say that the message should be written as a cartoon, not only in words. Others say that just leaving a message is not enough – there should also be a message about the message, asking that it be revised every two or three hundred years, so that it remains understandable for longer.

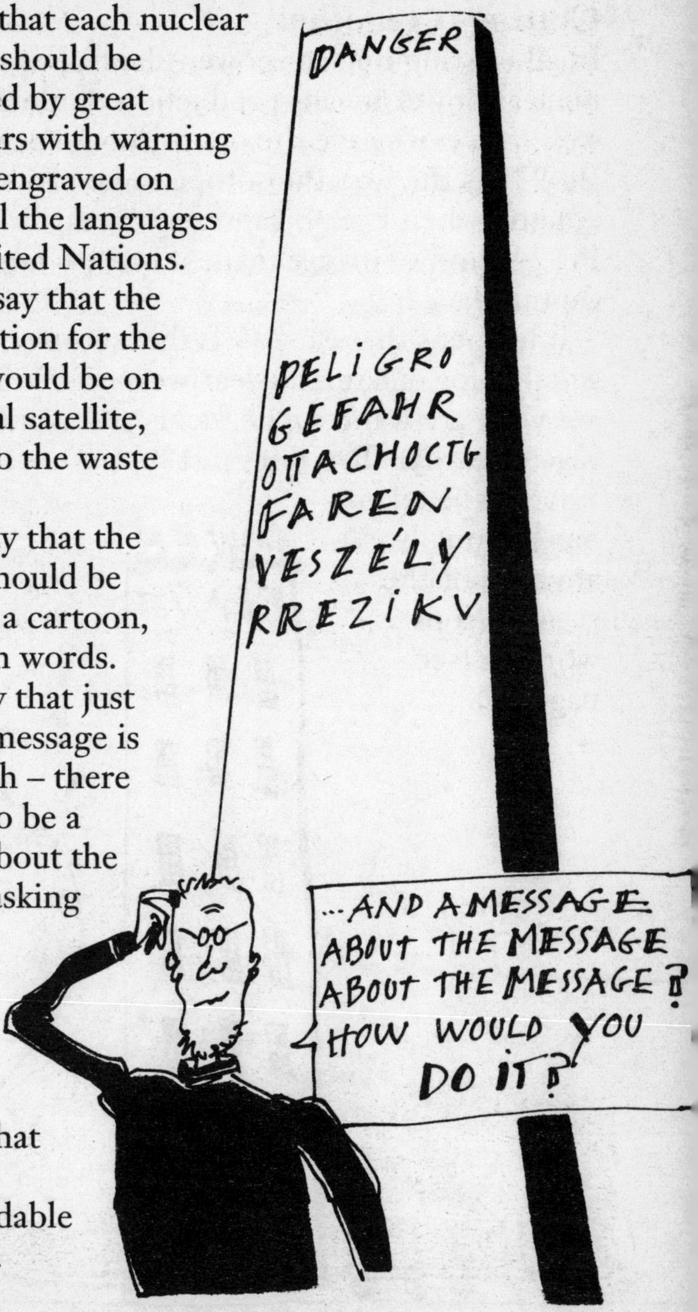

Getting it together

In all existing nuclear power plants, production of nuclear power means production of plutonium as well; you can't have the one without the other. Pu-239 is the first Pu isotope to be produced in a reactor, when U-238 captures a neutron. Pu-240, Pu-241 and so on are made if more neutrons are captured.

It happens that Pu-239 is the isotope most suitable for making nuclear weapons, so if weapons are what are wanted, the fuel is taken out of the reactor earlier than if it's just to make electricity. It has to be taken out eventually, anyhow, or the reactor stops working (see page 76).

How much you need for a bomb depends on how clever you are. Two kilos of Pu-239, 93% pure, is enough, if you know how. That's less than the size of a tennis ball. If you haven't any experience you might need four or five kilos. The difficult part is making the implosion to squash it together fast enough.

How a Pu bomb works

Yes, that's IMplosion, not EXplosion.

Not quite enough neutrons come out of ordinary plutonium to set off a bomb chain reaction.

But if the plutonium is squashed together hard enough and fast enough, the neutrons find fresh nuclei to fission just that much sooner, and the bomb works.

So you put a layer of high explosive all around the plutonium. The high explosive has to go off all at once. That's the difficult part.

It squashes the plutonium tighter together, which is why it's called an IMplosion. Then the plutonium EXplodes.

If you're satisfied with a comparatively small explosion then any old plutonium will do, whatever mixture of isotopes there is.

This means that anyone with the right engineering know-how who can get hold of a few kilograms of plutonium from a reactor can build a fearsome nuclear weapon.

And about thirty countries have nuclear reactors, while only five admit to having weapons (see page 50).

This is called the **proliferation** problem. It has got worse since the break-up of the Soviet Union because a lot of nuclear weapons are being dismantled, and the plutonium is not always being well looked after.

Since plutonium is very poisonous (see page 25), stolen plutonium could be very dangerous, just spread around in the atmosphere, even if it weren't made up into a bomb. International control would help.

How exactly does it kill you?

Nuclear radiation can break molecules apart. If this happens to molecules in a living cell, it can damage the cell, especially if a lot of molecules are affected all at once – cells are quite good at repairing damage which affects only a few molecules.

The effects of cell damage depend on which cells are damaged and how quickly this happens. Cells in bone marrow and in the small intestine are some of those that are most easily damaged. Bone marrow makes red blood cells to carry oxygen, white cells to fight infection, and platelets to stop bleeding. Without these you may die.

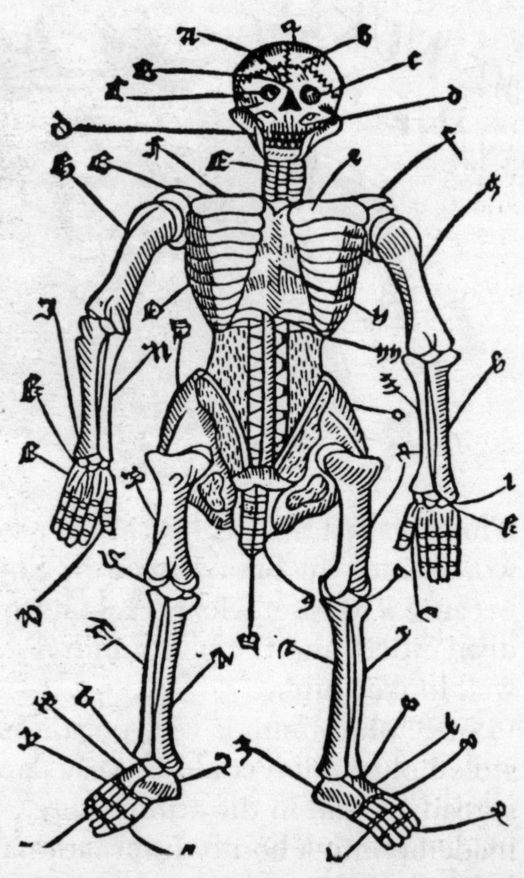

Radiation dose is measured in **Sieverts**, Sv for short. The dose depends on how much radiation energy is delivered to which part of the body, and on the kind of radiation – neutrons and α-rays are more damaging than β or γ-rays.

A 1 Sv dose to the whole body kills almost nobody. A 10 Sv dose to the whole body kills almost anybody within a few weeks.

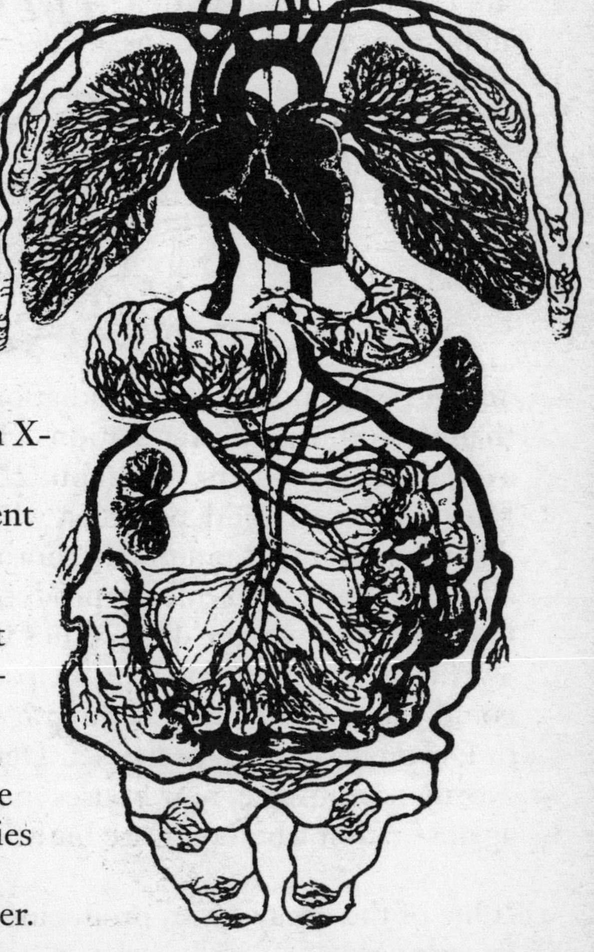

The UK average dose per person from nuclear power stations is 0.4 **μSv** a year. The UK average per person from X-rays and other medical treatment is nearly a thousand times as much – about 370 μSv a year – less than one two-thousandth of a Sievert. The annual dose varies a lot from one person to another.

Getting what comes naturally

You get a lot more nuclear radiation from nature than you do from power stations. In the UK the average dose per person is about 2210 μSv a year. How much you get depends on where you live. There's radium, uranium and thorium in rocks – in all rocks. Radioactive decay produces radon, a gas. Over half the average dose comes from radon.*

The gas can accumulate in a closed space. You could get cancer from breathing it. At some places in Devon, Cornwall, Somerset, Derbyshire and Northamptonshire, new houses must be protected against radon when they are built.

*One of the decay series producing radon is shown on page 31.

The Ra, Th and U from the rocks gets into the soil too, and then into your food. There's U in you! (Not much.)

Brazil nuts contain more radium than most other foods.

As for the rest – cosmic rays from outer space hit nuclei in the atmosphere and produce all kinds of radioactive stuff. There's more of it as you go up, so that people who live at high altitudes get a higher dose, and in only five air flights from the UK to Japan you could collect an extra 1,000 µSv or so.

Getting it straight

Let's get this straight. Plutonium is one of the most poisonous substances there is, nuclear power stations produce it in vast quantities, terrorists could kill thousands with a handful, and you want there to be MORE of all this?

What would you say about an invention that kills over 800,000 people a year and injures millions more, that produces nearly a quarter of the world's greenhouse gases and more air pollution than any other single activity?

I'm against it. What is it?

The main reason for wanting more nuclear power now is to help people in poor countries improve their lives without an enormous increase in the amount of greenhouse gases that are produced.

When other ways to produce energy are easily available and not too expensive, nuclear power can be given up.

How long will uranium last?

That depends on how it is used. In nearly all the reactors working now, the nuclear fuel is taken out before much of the uranium has been used up (see page 76).

The fuel is used in this way because the price of uranium is low – much lower than it used to be – so electricity companies see little reason to use it more efficiently if that involves higher costs.

It is estimated that known supplies of uranium would last at least until 2050 if they were used only in this way and at the same rate as they are now.

Nuclear fuel can be used about 60 times more efficiently than this, in *breeder reactors*. These reactors are called breeders because they are able to breed more nuclear fuel than they use up, by converting a lot of U-238 into Pu-239.

Another advantage of breeders is that they can use up most of the long half-life waste material that causes such difficult storage problems (see page 81).

If breeders were in widespread use, then known supplies of uranium could last for thousands of years.

In one design of breeder, called the *Integral Fast Reactor*, plutonium could be used in the place where it was made. This would make it more difficult to divert it to the making of nuclear weapons.

However, much more scientific and engineering work needs to be done before breeders can be widely used. The likely expense has put off companies and governments.

What about fusion?

Fission works for heavy nuclei – plutonium and uranium have atomic numbers 94 and 92. Fusion works best for light nuclei, such as hydrogen and helium isotopes, which have atomic numbers 1 and 2. When two light nuclei fuse, energy is released because the total mass of what comes out is less than the total mass of the bits it was made from.*

*See page 18.

The fusion process most hopeful for energy supply uses the hydrogen isotopes deuterium (D or $^{2}_{1}H$) and tritium (T or $^{3}_{1}H$).

The difficulty is that nuclei repel one another until they get really close, and to get them close you have to make them hot, so that they move fast and bang into each other hard.

The D-T mixture has to be made dense enough and hot enough – above 100 million °C – for long enough to produce more energy than has been used in heating the mixture. And the reactor where it's all happening mustn't melt!

Several methods have been tried, but so far, none has worked well enough to be usable for energy supply.

Fusion power 90% certain?

Sometimes someone thinks that he has a method that works.

January, 1958. Atomic Energy Research Establishment, at Harwell, near Oxford: Zero Energy Thermonuclear Assembly (ZETA) in operation.

Sir John Cockroft, Director: In this ZETA experiment, neutrons have been detected. I am ninety per cent certain that thermonuclear fusion is occurring.

May, 1958.

Announcement from Harwell: Sorry. Most of the neutrons detected were not the result of true thermonuclear reactions.

So it didn't work. Sometimes someone thinks that he can do it without the high temperature.

23 March 1989: University of Utah, Salt Lake City, Utah. Press conference held by Stanley Pons and Martin Fleischmann, professors of chemistry.

7 May 1989: Harwell. We have duplicated the experiments, using much more sensitive equipment. We should have seen something by now. We haven't.

So that didn't work either.

And fusion is still out of reach.

The wind, the Sun?

Total energy use in the world today is around 270 EJ (**exajoules**) a year. Total solar energy reaching the Earth's surface is about 4,500,000 EJ a year. About 1,300,000 EJ of this falls on land, the rest on the ocean. You would think that there was plenty to spare.

Apart from nuclear energy, nearly all the energy which humans use comes indirectly from the Sun to grow plants that are eaten, or burnt as biomass or fossil fuels, to drive the evaporation of water that is finally converted to hydropower, and to drive the winds that turn windmills.

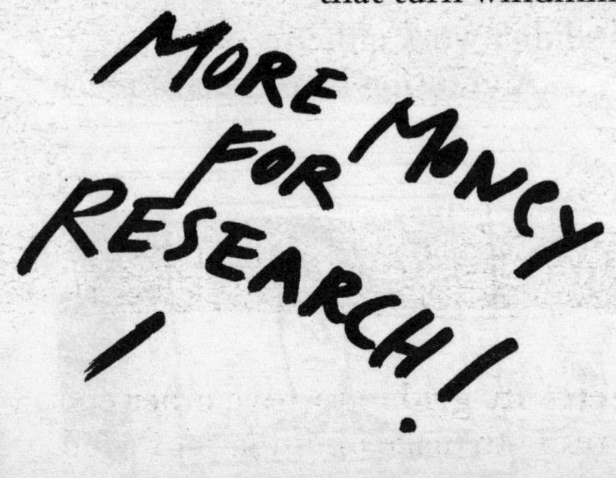

Nowadays wind power is used to make electricity, especially in Denmark and the US state of California; Denmark aims to make 10% of its electricity with wind power by 2005.

The windmills are spread out in large open spaces called 'wind farms'. The land between the windmills can be used for farming or ranching.

Some people object to the building of windmills in scenic countryside, others to the noise.

But wind power is not likely ever to produce a big share of world energy: a hopeful estimate of wind generated electricity in 2020 is only 3½ EJ.

The **electricity grid** must have other energy sources ready to make up for lack of wind.

Solar electricity

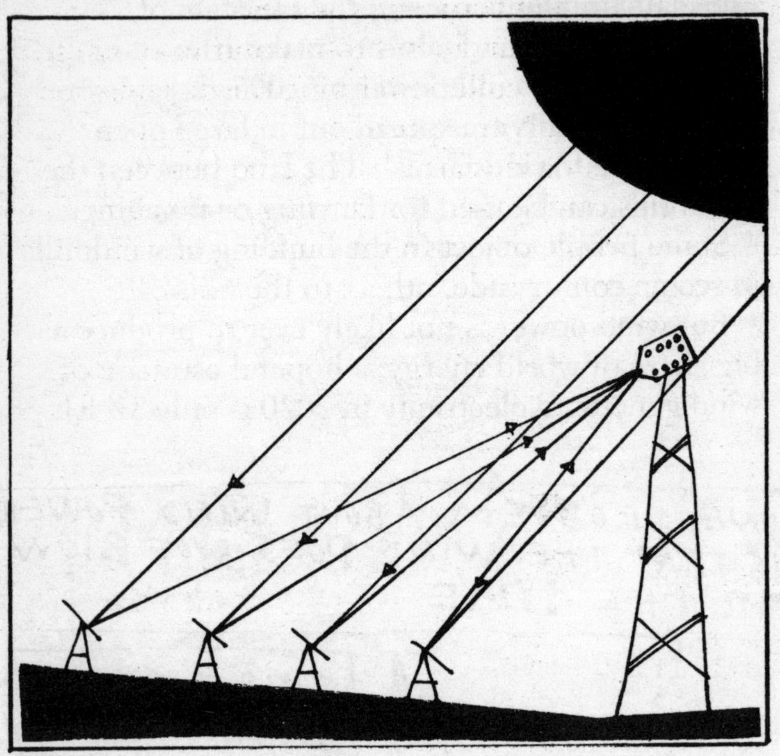

Electricity may be made using sunlight itself, without depending on wind or water.

One way is to use mirrors or lenses to concentrate the sunlight on a gas or liquid that is heated and drives a turbine, just as the heated gas or liquid in a nuclear reactor does.

The other way is to use what are called 'photovoltaic' (PV) systems that produce electricity directly from the sunlight.

PV systems can be built in all sizes, do not need much looking after, and do not produce any pollution while they are running.

PVs cost much more than other ways of making electricity, even in very sunny places.

And there's no sun at night. Intermittency again. The solar energy collected during the day must be stored somehow for use at night.

One way to do this is to have two reservoirs, one higher up than the other, and to pump water from the lower one to the higher one using solar energy. The water can be used later to drive turbines.

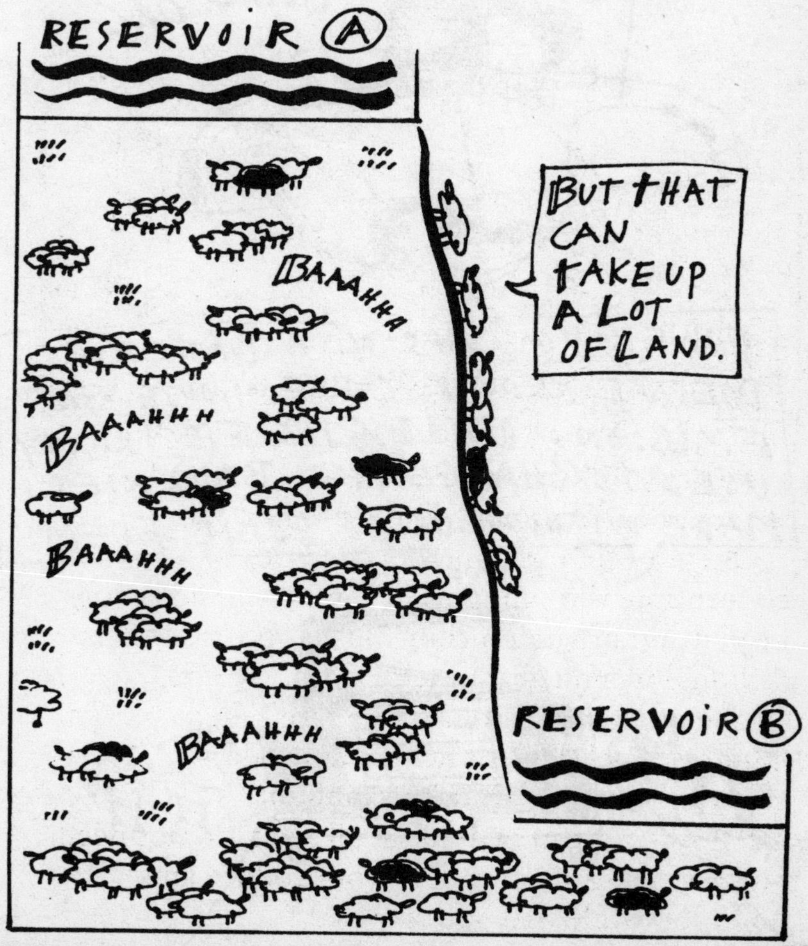

What about cars and trucks?

You can't run cars or trucks on electricity, or at least, not very well. Electric batteries for running cars are getting better, but they aren't powerful enough yet to be used easily outside cities.

Something needs to be done: in Britain, for example, CO_2 from road traffic is expected to increase by at least 40% from 1990 to 2025.

In the US there's one car to 1.7 people. In China it's one to 680 people – one four-hundredth as much.

One solution would be to run cars and other vehicles on hydrogen. The hydrogen could be made from water by a process using electricity made with nuclear power. Practically no carbon dioxide would be produced, and very little of other greenhouse gases – it wouldn't add to the Greenhouse problem.

Amplify your energy – safe nukes

The Italian physicist Carlo Rubbia has suggested that there could be an unexplodable nuclear reactor, which he calls the Energy Amplifier (EA). EAs would run on thorium (Th) instead of uranium.

Natural thorium is Th-232 ($^{232}_{90}$Th). It does not fission, but it can capture a neutron and turn into U-233, which does fission, and so give out some energy. However the fissioning of U-233 does not produce quite enough neutrons to keep the whole process going – some extra neutrons are needed.

That's why EAs would be unexplodable.

The necessary neutrons could be made by smashing a beam of protons into a target of molten lead (TCTE why this is a good way to do it). The beam of protons would come from a machine called an **accelerator.**

This may sound even more complicated than a reactor is, but one great advantage is that if you turned off the accelerator, the EA would soon stop.

What about thorium bombs – what about waste?

Another great advantage is that you can't make bombs out of thorium, because it doesn't produce enough neutrons to keep a chain reaction going.

You could reprocess the fuel and burn up nearly all the wastes in the EA itself. Depending on exactly what you decided to do, there could be about one-hundredth as much waste as from an old-fashioned reactor. No need for another Yucca Mountain. You could even use an EA to burn up some of the wastes from ordinary reactors.

You'll still need oil

You couldn't use an EA to run a car or a bus or a truck or a tractor. To start with, there would be about 10,000 tons of molten lead in it.

It's true that people are going to be using oil for quite a while, but later on EAs could be used to make hydrogen – and there's no Greenhouse Effect from hydrogen.

There aren't any EAs yet, because there's still a lot to be done, especially building a suitable accelerator. Money is needed for research, and to teach people how to run them properly.

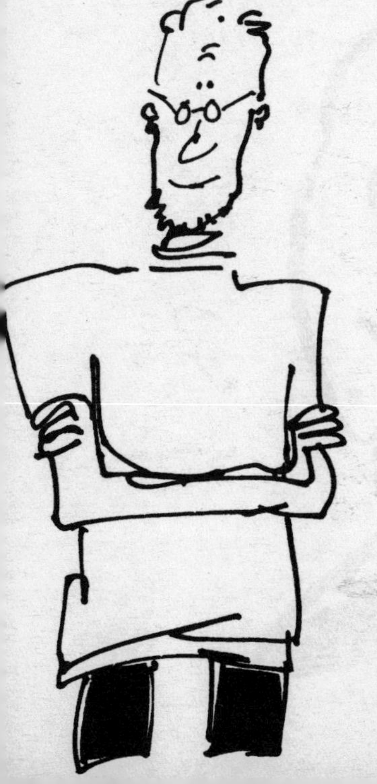

THERE COULD BE SOME SOON! AFTER ALL THERE'S NO UNDISCOVERED TECHNOLOGY INVOLVED – UNLIKE FLYING PIGS....

'So that's it. The world needs more energy, because there are poor people and there are going to be more people. Fossil fuels lead to the Greenhouse Effect; there aren't enough renewables; nuclear power doesn't lead to the Greenhouse Effect but it's dangerous if it's not looked after very carefully. You think that the answer is to have more nuclear power, and manage it properly.'

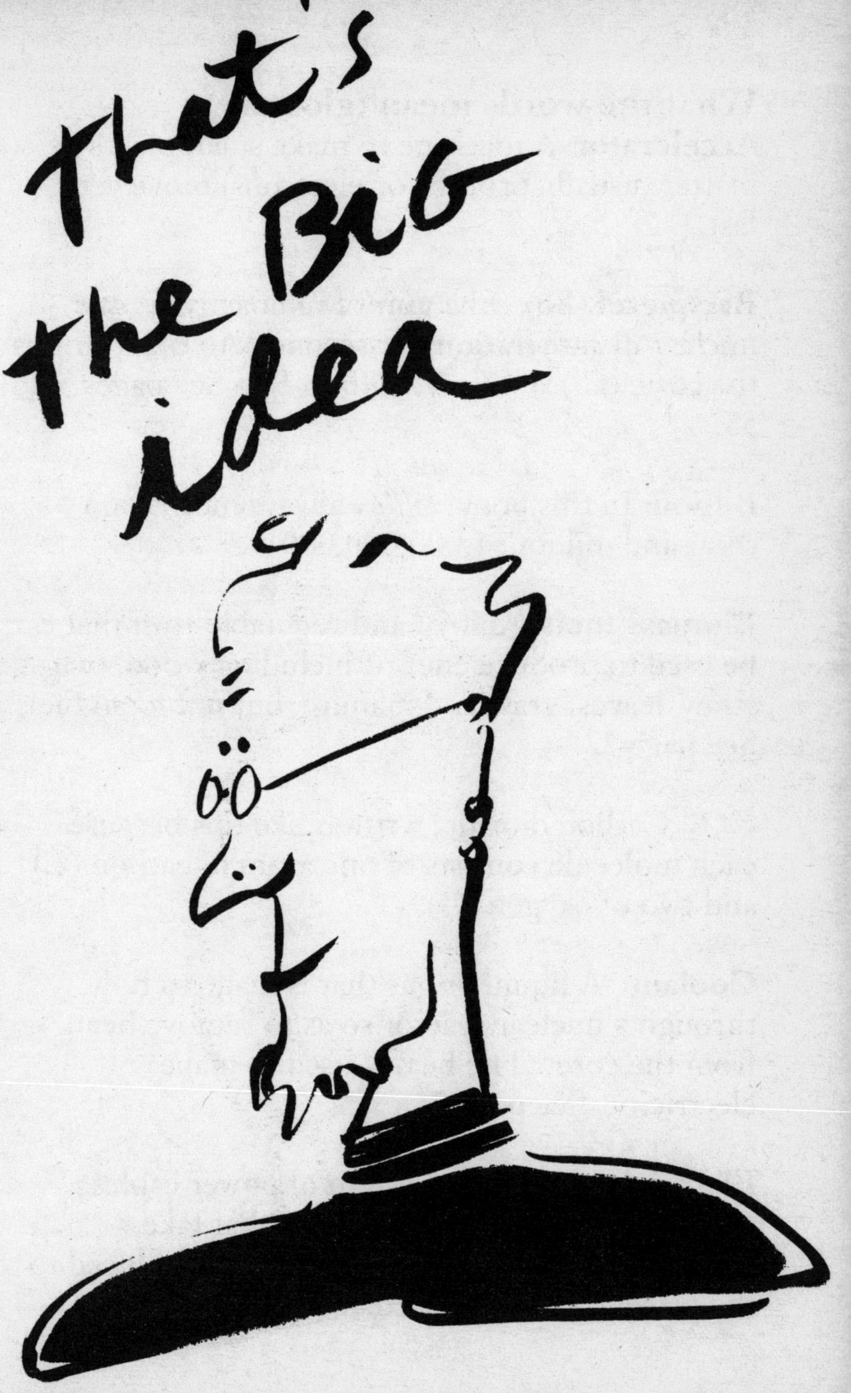

That's the BIG idea

What the words mean (glossary)

Accelerator: A machine to make small pieces of matter (usually protons or electrons) move very fast.

Becquerel (Bq): The unit of radioactivity: one nuclear disintegration per second. An older unit is the curie (Ci): 1 Ci = 37 billion Bq. See pages 52, 55.

Billion: In this book, *billion* always means one thousand million: 1,000,000,000.

Biomass fuels: Animal and vegetable stuff that can be used to produce energy, including wood, twigs, straw, leaves, grass and manure, but not fossil fuels. See page 72.

CO_2: Carbon dioxide, written like this because each molecule consists of one atom of carbon (C) and two of oxygen (O).

Coolant: A liquid or gas that is made to flow through a nuclear reactor so as to remove heat from the core. The heat is used to make electricity. See page 75.

Electricity grid: The system of power cables, wires, transformers and switches that take electricity from the places where it is produced to the places where it is used. See page 103.

Element: Matter consisting of atoms each of whose nuclei contains the same number of protons. For example, the element uranium consists of atoms each of whose nuclei contains 92 protons.

Fossil fuels: formed over periods of many thousand years by gradual change in remains of dead plants and animals. Burning them produces CO_2, adding to the Greenhouse Effect. See pages 12 (for energy production), 17, 64 (for the Greenhouse Effect), and 72 (for limited supplies).

Exajoule: see Joule.

Gigajoule: see Joule.

Greenhouse Effect: Warming of the Earth's atmosphere by trapping of more of the Sun's heat, partly as a result of human activities. See pages 64-71.

Half-life: The time it takes for half of a quantity of any particular radioactive isotope to turn into something else. See page 31.

High level waste: In the UK, radioactive waste producing enough heat that storage must be designed to allow for this. See page 77.

Isotope: Nuclei of a particular element with different numbers of neutrons (so that they have different mass numbers) are called isotopes of that element. See page 24.

Joule: The joule (J) is a unit of energy. One joule per second is one watt, so a one-kilowatt electric fire sends out 1,000 joules of heat energy each second.
1,000 J = 1 kilojoule (kJ)
1,000 kJ = 1 megajoule (MJ) = 10^6 J
1,000 MJ = 1 gigajoule (GJ) = 10^9 J
1,000 GJ = 1 terajoule (TJ) = 10^{12} J
1,000 TJ = 1 petajoule (PJ) = 10^{15} J
1,000 PJ = 1 exajoule (EJ) = 10^{18} J.

Mass: A measure of the amount of material in something. At any particular place, the weight of a thing is a measure of the mass, but the weight is different in different places: for example, the weight of a thing on the Moon would be only about one-sixth of the weight of that same thing on the Earth, but the mass is the same everywhere. How mass is lost when nuclear energy is produced is explained on page 18.

Microgram: one millionth of a gram.

Nuclear reactor: A machine for producing heat energy by the fission or fusion of atomic nuclei. See page 17 (fission) and page 98 (fusion).

Proliferation: The spread of nuclear weapons to more countries. Some people think it is a bad thing that more countries should have nuclear weapons than do already. Others think it is a bad thing that any country should have them. See page 89.

Radiation: To radiate means to send out something. Nuclei radiate α-rays, β-rays and γ-rays, which are explained on page 30. Some nuclei also send out neutrons. Besides γ-rays, *electromagnetic radiation* includes ordinary light, ultraviolet and infrared rays, radio waves and X-rays. See page 30.

Radioactive: Any material containing nuclei that send out radiation.

Sievert: The unit of absorbed radiation dose, taking into account the biological damage done by different kinds of radiation.

1 mSv (milliSievert) = 1/1,000 Sv
1 μSv (microSievert)= 1/1,000,000 Sv

TCTE: Too Complicated To Explain, usually because it would take a lot of maths, and more space than there is to spare in this book.

TNT: Trinitrotoluene, an explosive. See page 19.

Ton: In this book, ton always means a metric ton, or tonne, of 1,000 kilograms.

Who's who

Becquerel, Antoine Henri (1852-1908) French physicist. Discovered radioactivity. Page 28.

Curie, Irène Joliot (1897-1956), French physicist, daughter of Pierre and Marie Curie, with her husband *Frédéric Joliot*, (1900-1958) discovered artificial radioactivity. Page 32.

Curie, Marie Sklodowska (1867-1934, Polish-born) and *Pierre Curie* (1859-1906). French physicists, wife and husband. Discovered radium and polonium. Page 29.

Einstein, Albert (1879-1955) German-born physicist, worked in Switzerland and the US. Famous for his theories of relativity. Page 18.

Eisenhower, Dwight David (1890-1969) General commanding the invasion of the Continent from Britain on 6 June 1944; President of the US 1952-1956. Page 47.

Fermi, Enrico (1901-1954) Italian-born physicist, worked also in the US. Constructed the first nuclear reactor. Pages 33, 36 and 39.

Franck, James (1882-1964) German born physicist, worked also in the US. Head of a committee which suggested that atomic bombs should not be used against Japan. Page 43.

Frisch, Otto Robert (1904-1979) and *Lise Meitner* (1878-1968), Austrian born physicists, nephew and aunt. Working together, first to understand fission. Pages 34 and 35.

Groves, General Leslie (1896-1970). Military head of the Manhattan Project for atom bomb development. Pages 38-43.

Hahn, Otto (1879-1968) German physicist and chemist. Working with *Fritz Strassmann* (1902-1980), discovered nuclear fission. Page 33.
Klaproth, Martin Heinrich (1743-1817) German chemist. Discovered uranium. Page 28.
Lawrence, Ernest Orlando (1901-1958) American physicist, invented new ways to make radioactivity, worked on Manhattan Project. Page 42.
Oppenheimer, Julius Robert (1904-1967) American physicist. Director of the atom bomb project at Los Alamos, New Mexico, 1942-1945. Page 38.
Rubbia, Carlo (1934-). Italian physicist. Suggested the Energy Amplifier. Page 108.
Rutherford, Ernest (1871-1937) New Zealand-born physicist, who worked in Canada and England. Sorted out α, β and γ-rays (page 30), and explained atom as nucleus surrounded by electrons (see page 21).
Stimson, Henry Lewis (1867-1950) American politician; Secretary of War 1940-1945. Page 41.
Szilard, Leo (1898-1964) Hungarian born physicist, worked also in Germany and the US. Page 36.

Books for more information

There is more about the science of nuclear power in *The Dorling Kindersley Science Encyclopedia*, *The Oxford Children's Book of Science*, *The Usborne Illustrated Dictionary of Science*, and in David Macaulay's *The Way Things Work*, and Philip Wilkinson's *Super Structures*, both Dorling Kindersley books.

Simple explanations of the different kinds of nuclear reactors can be found in Guy Arnold's *Facts on Nuclear Energy*, a Gloucester Press book or in *Finding Out about Nuclear Energy*, published by Hobson Ltd. These two are both out of print, but might be found in libraries.

There are hundreds of more specialised adult books on all the subjects of this book. Among standard books the following may be useful for reference:

Arnold, Lorna *Windscale 1957: Anatomy of a Nuclear Accident*, Macmillan, 1992. Official history.

Cole, H. A. *Understanding Nuclear Power: A technical guide to the industry and its processes*, Gower Technical Press, 1988. One of hundreds, but clearer than most. Some details about the British nuclear programme now out of date.

Glasstone, Samuel and Philip J Dolan, compilers *The Effects of Nuclear Weapons*, Third Edition, 1977, US Departments of Defense and Energy. Incudes a Bomb Effects Computer.

Houghton, J and others, editors, *Climate Change 1995: The Science of Climate Change; Impacts, Adaptations and Mitigation of Climate Change; Economic and Social Dimensions of Climate Change*. Cambridge University Press 1996. Everything about the Greenhouse Effect and what can be done to reduce it.

Johansson, Thomas B, Henry Kelly, A K N Reddy and R H Williams *Renewable Energy*, Earthscan/Island Press, 1993. Details of wind, solar, biomass, hydro. Rather optimistic about future prospects.

Mould, R F *Chernobyl: the Real Story* Pergamon 1988. Lots of pictures.

World Energy Council WEC Commission: *Energy for Tomorrow's World*, Kogan Page, 1993. Estimates of how much will be needed in the 21st century.

World Resources: 1996-97, Oxford University Press, 1996. Country-by-country details of population, food, forests, energy use, national income, water, climate.

Internet sites

These are a few among the hundreds of sites with data or discussion about nuclear power and ideas having to do with it. They are chosen because they have useful information; some of them are for nuclear power, some against it, some just informative.

British Nuclear Fuels Limited (BNFL): details of nuclear sites in UK: http://www.bnfl.com

Environmental Organization Web Directory, including Solar Energy, Conservation, Air Pollution, Hazardous Waste, Sustainable Development: http://www.webdirectory.com

Nuclear Fusion: 'An Explanation Even My Mother Understands': http://www.ceas.rochester.edu:8080/ee/users/kgreen/pages/fusion1.html

GreenNet (UK): for the Environment, Peace and Human Rights: http://www.gn.apc.org

Greenpeace (seeks to protect biodiversity in all its forms, prevent pollution and abuse of the earth's ocean, land, air and fresh water, end all nuclear threats, promote peace, global disarmament and nonviolence): http://www.greenpeace.org

Intergovernmental Panel on Climate Change: (IPCC): http://www.unep.ch/ipcc/ipcc-0.html

International Atomic Energy Agency (IAEA) of the United Nations system: especially FACTS & FIGURES including Nuclear Power By Country : http://www.iaea.or.at

N-BASE (Nuclear Information Service, based in the Shetland Islands: database plus news and analysis on the UK civil nuclear industry, particularly reprocessing, nuclear transports, waste and marine pollution): http://www.zetnet.co.uk/oigs/n-base/home.htm

Natural Resources Defense Council (US) (has issue indexes, including air, agriculture, drinking water, energy, garbage, global warming, health, nuclear, oceans, transportation): http://www.nrdc.org/nrdc

NIREX UK radioactive waste management: http://www.nirex.co.uk

Nuclear Control Institute (NCI) (US) (an independent research and advocacy center specializing in problems of nuclear proliferation. Material includes: The Plutonium Threat, The Bomb-Grade Uranium Threat, Nuclear Disarmament, Nuclear Terrorism): http://www.wideopen.igc.org/nci/index.htm

Nuclear Encyberpaedia of British Nuclear Industry Forum: 12 chapters on nuclear physics, nuclear power, British programmes, + glossary: http://www.encyberpedia.com/ency.htm

Nuclear Energy Agency of the Organisation for Economic Cooperation and Development (OECD): http://www.nea.fr

Nuclear Energy Institute (NEI) is the nuclear energy industry's Washington based policy organization. http://www.nei.org/

Nuclear Information World Wide Web Server: large collection of info, including World Nuclear Power Plant Information: http://nuke.handheld.com/

Nuclear Weapons: Frequently Asked Questions: http://www.pal.xgw.fi/hew/NFAQ0.HTML

NucNet: the World's Nuclear News Agency of the European Nuclear Society (ENS): http://www.aey.ch/nucnet

Rocky Mountain Institute (works for a blend of efficient energy use with appropriate renewable sources): http://www.rmi.org

United Kingdom Atomic Energy Authority (UKAEA): (waste disposal; nuclear fuel reprocessing; fusion): http://www.ukaea.org.uk/about/index.htm

United Nations Environment Programme (UNEP): http://www.unep.org

Uranium Information Centre Melbourne, Australia, especially the Nuclear Issues Briefing Papers: http://www.uic.com.au/index.htm

Uranium Institute, London: Information about the Civil Nuclear Industry Nuclear FAQs & Figures Glossary of Nuclear terms. Link to other Nuclear Industy WWW sites: http://www.uilondon.org/uihome.html

US Department of Energy, especially Energy Information Administration, for example http://www.eia.doe.gov/fuelnonfossil.html

World Resources Institute (US): available data includes Development and Environment, Climate, Energy and Pollution, Economics and Population, Technology and the Environment: http://www.wri.org/wri/wri.html

Yucca Mountain Project: http://www.ymp.gov

Index

Neither words in *What the Words Mean* (pages 114-117) nor people in *Who's Who* (pages 118-119) are listed in this Index.

alpha rays 30
atomic bomb 37-45
atomic number 22
atoms, size of 21
beta rays 30
brazil nuts, radium in 93
carbon dioxide (CO_2) 66
cells, radiation damage to 90
chain reaction, first 39
Chernobyl, accident at 54-57
deuterium 46, 99
Einstein's formula
for mass loss 18
Energy Amplifier (EA) 108-111
fossil fuels, using up of 72
gamma rays 30
global warming 67-69
Hiroshima and Nagasaki,
destruction of 44-45
HLW, ILW, LLW 77-80
hydrogen bomb 46
tests of 47
iodine tablets,
distribution of 57
iodine-131, danger of 52, 57
Manhattan Project 38
mass number 22
neptunium,
first manufacture of 38
neutron 16
nuclear fission, discovery of 34
nuclear power plant,
first British 48
nuclear radiation,
danger of 55, 92
nuclear transformations 29-31
nuclear waste, storage of 76-85
nuclear weapons,
countries owning 50
use of 44-45
nucleon 16
plutonium, dangers of 25
first manufacture of 38
isotopes of 86
plutonium bombs,
design of 86-87
polonium, discovery of 29
proton 16
radiation doses 90-93
radioactivity, discovery of 28
radium, discovery of 29
thorium, use in reactors 108
Three Mile Island,
accident at 58
tritium 46, 99
uranium, discovery of 28
isotopes of 23
wind power 103
Windscale, accident at 52
Yucca Mountain 83

THANK YOU FOR HELPING

Nadine Ballantyne (Crown Woods School), Dr Martin Birnstingl, Sir Hermann Bondi, Dr Federico Carminati (CERN), Mr James Hanlon, Harry Johns (Hendon School), Emma and Sarah Lewis (Oxford High School), Harman Mattu (Westminster School), Dr Marta Monteleoni, Donna Nixon (Hackbridge Junior School), Captain Chris Roper, Emma Vallance, Mrs Denie Weil, Mr Frank Weil, Ben Westoby (University College School), and Professor Maurice Wilkins (Nobel Laureate) were kind and patient enough to read and comment on the text before there were any pictures. What errors and misrepresentations remain are of course the author's fault.

The author acknowledges with thanks the help of the American Airpower Heritage Museum, Midland, Texas, whose Director permitted him to quote from the Museum's Web page the text of Col. Paul Tibbets reproduced on page 45.

Special thanks to Margaret Conroy, Anna Davidson and Steve Wilson for all their help.

ORDER FORM

WHAT'S THE BIG IDEA?

0 304 722630	Alien Life	£3.99	☐
0 304 667206	Animal Rights	£3.99	☐
0 304 67847X	The Environment	£3.99	☐
0 304 724056	Food*	£3.99	☐
0 304 708778	Genetics	£3.99	☐
0 304 722916	The Media*	£3.99	☐
0 304 655887	The Mind	£3.99	☐
0 304 693398	Nuclear Power	£3.99	☐
0 304 714824	The Paranormal*	£3.99	☐
0 304 667192	Religion	£3.99	☐
0 304 655909	Time and the Universe	£3.99	☐
0 304 655917	Virtual Reality	£3.99	☐
0 304 655895	Women's Rights	£3.99	☐

* coming soon

Books in this series are available at your local bookshop, or can be ordered direct from the publisher. A complete list of titles is given above. Just tick the titles you would like and complete the details below. Prices and availability are subject to change without prior notice.

Please enclose a cheque or postal order made payable to Bookpoint Ltd, and send to: Hodder Children's Books, Cash Sales Dept, Bookpoint, 39 Milton Park, Abingdon, Oxon OX14 4TD. Email address: orders@bookpoint.co.uk.

If you would prefer to pay by credit card, our call centre team would be delighted to take your order by telephone. Our direct line is 01235 400414 (lines open 9.00 am – 6.00 pm, Monday to Saturday; 24 hour message answering service). Alternatively you can send a fax on 01235 400454.

Title .... First name .... Surname ....

Address ....

....

....

Daytime tel .... Postcode ....

If you would prefer to post a credit card order, please complete the following.

Please debit my Visa/Access/Diners Card/American Express (delete as applicable) card number:

Signature .... Expiry Date ....

If you would NOT like to receive further information on our products, please tick ☐